SELIG PERLMAN'S
Lectures on Capitalism and Socialism

SELIG PERLMAN'S
Lectures on
Capitalism
and Socialism

A. L. RIESCH OWEN

The University of Wisconsin Press

The publication of this book
has been made possible
with the assistance of the
John R. Commons Fund

Published 1976

The University of Wisconsin Press
Box 1379, Madison, Wisconsin 53701

The University of Wisconsin Press, Ltd.
70 Great Russell Street, London

First printing

Printed in the United States of America

For LC CIP information see the colophon

ISBN 0-299-06780-7

To my parents
Amelia and Louis Riesch, Sr.

Contents

Foreword

The University of Wisconsin's Announcement of Courses, 1929–30, indicated
that the course in the Economics Department entitled "Capitalism and Socialism," hitherto taught by John R. Commons, was now to be part of the teaching
program of Selig Perlman, who had become a full professor in 1927. Although
Professor Perlman always acknowledged his personal and intellectual indebtedness to John R. Commons, we can be sure that the course familiarly known as
Cap-Soc was very much his own. He continued to teach this course, which
attracted students from almost every part of the University, many parts of the
country, and, indeed, the world. In 1941–42, the year that Anna Lou Riesch,
a candidate for the Ph.D. in History, took Economics 144 as part of the Minor
requirement, Professor Perlman succinctly summarized what he was doing:
"Capitalism, Unionism, Socialism, Fascism, and Individualistic Anti-Capital-
ism, each viewed under the headings of conditions, theories, and movements."
The prerequisites were Economics 1a and senior standing.

Somewhat in the manner of the more conscientious and painstaking students
in medieval universities, Miss Riesch (now Mrs. Wyn Owen) took excellent
notes. She studied with Professor Perlman throughout her graduate training,
and her later professional experience at several universities has enabled her to
present the Perlman material in a meaningful form. The notes Dr. Owen took
as a student she has now edited and prepared with the background of a professor and a continuing personal friendship with Professor Perlman. While retaining the flavor of Professor Perlman and his originality of thought by using
the first person in the presentation of the lectures, Dr. Owen's contributions
are significant in that she has put the material together and hence made it
relevant to current movements of thought. The text of the lectures is com-
parable to similar ventures in the world of scholarship, such, for example, as
the published notes of courses taught at Columbia by Wesley Mitchell and at
Chicago by George Herbert Mead. It was fortunate that Miss Riesch included
Professor Perlman's comments, in the discussion groups, on the basic readings
required of everyone and also on books on which students made special reports. The inclusion of Professor Perlman's examinations given in the course
further illustrate and illuminate his teaching objectives and techniques.

The publication of the lectures is justifiable on several grounds. They illuminate the scholarship in a relatively new and growing field at a critical point

in its development. They reflect, both in their affirmations and in their criticisms, many components in the climate of opinion of the late 1930s and early 1940s. It is also clear that a good deal in the lectures is relevant to many issues and interests in our own day.

In the first place, Professor Perlman's exposition of Marxist-Leninist theory reflects a deep understanding, resting on his own early commitment to it as a young man in Czarist Russia and in Naples, where he pursured an education denied him in his homeland, and on his own subsequent experiences as a leading figure in labor economics and action in the United States and as a participant in several civic and humanitarian movements. Having given up doctrinaire Marxism, he did not, as was true of many of his contemporaries, throw the baby out with the bath. His criticisms of Marxist-Leninist theory were balanced by an appreciation of its important contributions in the history of thought and action; and he urged his students to be sensitive to the need for continuing Marx's method of social analysis.

In Professor Perlman's view this could in part be done by analytical comparisons of Marxist-Leninist theory with competing theories. It could also be done by constructing hypotheses and then testing these with an empirical consideration of what one would expect on the basis of these hypotheses to find and then of what one actually did find—with shrewd and often original explanations. Suspicious of abstractions, Perlman's commitment to institutional economics and instrumentalist philosophy led him to examine, with learning and detachment, groups within economic groups, no less than political, military, and professional and intellectual groups, to take into account the values of these and their actual behavior in terms of multiple crosscurrents and complex motives and contingencies. In a true sense, therefore, he anticipated many of the presuppositions and concepts, it not all the methods, of the behavioral scientists of our time.

Considering, as he did, ideas and movements of thought in a cultural context of continuity and change, Professor Perlman was, in these lectures, as much a historian as an economic theorist; indeed, in his view, the two could not be properly or fruitfully separated. But he was not merely a conventional historian. Long before the current interest in comparative history, Perlman was comparing revolutionary movements, institutions, political parties and behavior, and "national character" itself, in several countries, notably Russia, Western Europe and Britain, the United States, Japan and China. These comparisons were informed, judicious, imaginative, and realistically empirical. A central concern in these analyses was the problem of power within social structure. This concern helps to explain the relevance of the lectures to a major issue in contemporary social science investigation and discussion.

The lectures also seem to me important because, instead of merely assuming, as so many historians did, and do, that students would by and of themselves see the bearing of historical data and explanation on the issues of their own day, Professor Perlman skillfully related his analyses of the past to current interests. These included Nazism, anti-Semitism, and the New Deal, especially its bearing on the question of whether or not the United States in its development, experiences, and immediate future did or did not demonstrate the theory of "exceptionalism." Even more specifically, the lectures not infrequently reflected a thoughtful acquaintance with new and much discussed books and writings in several languages as well as with current government reports and even special feature articles in the *New York Times.*

All this would make the lectures well worth reading for their substantive and methodological value, and their relevance to much that concerns us today. But in addition, the often brilliant analogies, homespun humor, metaphors and proverbs, and, above all, the warmth of human understanding combined with detachment, which characterized Professor Perlman's personality and mind, live for us again.

Professor Perlman once told me that there were those who were somewhat critical of him for not continuing to produce research monographs such as his early books. He did, to be sure, continue to write, and what he wrote reflected his penetrating mind and his familiarity with events and with scholarship in his field. He went on, as I recall, to add that he put a great deal of his research into his teaching. I believe that these lectures, in one of the most justly famous courses in the history of the University of Wisconsin, demonstrate the truth of this remark and help us to understand Selig Perlman's distinction as a historical thinker and his greatness as a teacher.

Merle Curti

Preface

Perhaps because of the man himself as well as his unique background, Professor Selig Perlman brought an unusual combination of qualities to his classroom. Never were his lectures lacking as a source of stimulation and challenge. Speaking from personal exposure and knowledge, he gave a richness, originality, and vividness to provocative material that encouraged his students in the development of intellectual inquiry and analysis.

Selig Perlman was born in 1888 in Bialystok, Poland, then a part of Czarist Russia. As the son of a yarn spinner and member of a persecuted minority, he grew up in an environment of revolutionary ferment that embraced the labor movement, socialism, and Zionism. In order to further his education, Perlman attended the University of Naples in 1906-7. While in Italy he met Mr. and Mrs. William English Walling, prominent American Socialists, who were instrumental in his coming to the United States in 1908.

Perlman was a Socialist when he arrived in the United States—an avowed Marxist. At the age of twenty he became a student of Professor John R. Commons at the University of Wisconsin, beginning a time of life spent primarily in Madison. He soon became Commons' research assistant and under his mentor's tutelage earned his A.B. degree in 1910 and his Ph.D. in 1915. Perlman became an American citizen in 1913 and continued his academic career as a faculty member at the University of Wisconsin, advancing through the ranks from instructor in 1919 to professor in 1927. At the culmination of his career, Professor Perlman had devoted better than forty years of service to the state of Wisconsin.

Perlman's association with Professor Commons was both academic and personal, and the influence of his teacher and friend had a profound effect in shaping Perlman's life and thought. It was an influence often acknowledged, particularly in Perlman's frequent references to the Commons-Perlman theory of the labor movement. Certainly Professor Commons encouraged his protégé in the development of a theory of the American labor movement, but it was Perlman's theory, growing out of his own study, background, and reflection.

The realization that politics was not a mere reflection of economics led Perlman to question and challenge Karl Marx. He found that politics exists independently of economics, a fact that did not detract from the importance of economics. Although he was grateful to the study of Marxism for the development of his mental capacities, Perlman became convinced that one should go beyond abstract concepts in the formulation of theories. He believed Marx was ahead of his time in projecting realism into historical thinking; however, Perlman insisted that it was essential to study the conduct of groups in actual life in order to understand the motivating forces at work.

Perlman could not believe, as Marx did, that the play had been written many years earlier and that an attempt to learn what the individual actor was thinking would prove fruitless. Perlman's interpretation placed the concrete person in the center of the stage. The actor was not interested in the making of history but concerned himself with day-to-day recognition and the improvement of his role both materially and spiritually.

Work with Socialists in the United States intensified Perlman's conviction that a concrete approach to economics was highly important. His research led to his job-conscious thesis, a turning point in Perlman's thinking about the labor movement—the concrete point of view triumphed over the abstract.

There were other respects in which Perlman could not follow Karl Marx. For one, he objected to the oversimplification Marx espoused in the materialistic conception of history based on the assumption that the struggle of economic classes was the only history-making entity. Perlman had observed that political groups could make history as well.

Perlman was the product of a certain period in the development of economic thought. As a man and a scholar he experienced both the economics of communism and the economics of a noncommunist country moving through a great depression. He was, above all, a labor historian and philosopher. As such he began teaching the course entitled "Capitalism and Socialism," in 1928, in the Department of Economics at the University of Wisconsin. The richness of his background and his own warmth of personality and willingness to spend countless hours in conference with his students made the courses he taught among the most popular on the campus. Cap–Soc attracted students of widely differing backgrounds and specializations.

Of all his courses, "Capitalism and Socialism" was, perhaps, the most original. Its timeliness, including both the past and the present, made it an always contemporary offering. Its broad content in economics, history, political science, sociology, and even psychology still warrants the attention of social scientists, and it was presented by a master of social analysis and creative synthesis.

This book is written with a view to making the content and style of presentation of this exciting class available to contemporary students.

"Capitalism and Socialism" was presented as a lecture-discussion course. Lectures were expanded by regularly held graduate discussions based on assigned readings and oral reports and were directed by Professor Perlman personally.

The book is based on four sources. (1) Detailed lecture notes I took as a student in 1942 were fully utilized. Although not verbatim and not transcribed shorthand notes, they are offered as a close approximation to Perlman's presentation—not as a conventional editing but rather as a meticulous writing and rewriting of the lectures and discussions based both on my own notes and on further research as indicated, as well as on my close personal relationship with Professor Perlman. (2) The lecture notes and discussion notes are complemented by my own research while a student in the course and through my lecture preparation over the years as a university teacher. (3) Supplementary research was completed while preparing this manuscript. (4) Other student lecture notes were available which enabled me to check the validity and content of my own notes, and I had the benefit of comments and reactions of other Perlman students. These sources and background have enabled me to rework the lectures and discussions which form the substance of the book. Certain discussions conducted by Professor Perlman enriched specific lectures, although they were primarily based upon assignments for outside reading. These offer a means of rounding out Perlman's concepts by his relevant observations and judgments. My discussion notes have been added as guides to the assignments, and footnotes for clarification.

As far as possible I have tried to inject into the lecture presentations and discussions Professor Perlman's lively style and manner of delivery. To this end I have used the first person in preparing my version of his lectures and discussions. I hope the reader will experience some of the excitement, discovery, and sense of intellectual adventure felt by me and countless other Perlman students who attended his course.

I should like to express my gratitude to the many who have made this work possible. My deep appreciation should not be minimized by the fact that space does not allow me to name each one individually.

As a former student of Professor Merle Curti, I would like to express my admiration and appreciation to a scholar and teacher who has been influential in my professional and personal life, as he has been to many others, in the setting of high standards and stimulation in dealing with ideas. The discipline of endless research and questioning, analysis and synthesis has stood me in good stead in this venture. Especially, I wish to thank him for the Foreword he has written to this volume.

My gratitude is extended to Mrs. Selig Perlman and her son, Professor Mark Perlman, for their initial permission and approval of this undertaking. I am particularly indebted to Professor Mark Perlman for the time he has taken to give a careful and critical reading to the completed manuscript and for his endorsement of the book.

I am also grateful to have had Chancellor Edwin Young entrust me with his set of lecture notes for Cap–Soc, taken in 1943 when he was a student in Selig

Perlman's class. Those notes were not incorporated into the manuscript but were valuable in checking various points and determining the accuracy of my own notes.

Also, particular thanks are extended to Professor Manuel Sigüenza, Professor of Economics, Graduate School of Business Administration, University of Puerto Rico. His never-ending enthusiasm and interest have been sources of constant encouragement. In addition, he read the entire manuscript and made constructive comments that have been most helpful. Another colleague who spent countless hours in reading the manuscript, Professor Jack Garlington, gave it the best of meticulous criticism. I am also indebted to Professor Homer Rainey for his help and support in innumerable ways. Genevieve Winchester and Dorothea El Mallakh have made valuable suggestions and criticisms as well as given constructive assistance.

I am most appreciative of my typist, Eloise Pearson, who not only typed several drafts, but was an invaluable assistant in many ways. Her countless hours of labor and valuable criticism and personal interest have been very important.

Above all, I would like to thank my immediate family, my husband, Wyn, and especially my children, Deann, Todd, and John, who have given me their full cooperation and understanding as well as those precious periods of silence when I needed them.

Numerous friends and colleagues as well as former students of Professor Perlman and my own students have all helped to make this work possible.

A. L. Riesch Owen

MARXIST THEORY

PART ONE
Intellectual Certainties

LECTURE 1
Some Certainties Upset

"Capitalism and Socialism," as the title of this course, takes up revolutionary theory and movements, and labor movements in general. It begins in the middle of the nineteenth century and goes to the present.

I was a student in Russia and was interested in my work and field in 1904-5. Going back, I find that there were interesting things we took for certainties. Now, I will deal rather with possibilities and probabilities. I no longer insist on certainties.

PERIOD OF THE FIRST RUSSIAN REVOLUTION

What were considered as established certainties? (1) It was considered thirty-five years ago that the existing order of things—the capitalistic system (ownership and private enterprise)—was just a historical phase, a phase of development in society. It set a tone to the thinking. We got our line of thought from Marx. We were positive that the nineteenth century would not stand still, that the social system was bound to change. (2) Capitalistic society was seen as divided into two camps—two opposite poles in society. At one pole, big business—finance—those who managed and those who depended on business. The other camp, the camp of the proletariat—wage earners—who, under the impact of capitalism, were bound to foregather for the purpose of revolution—they would abolish capitalism and institute a new type of society dominated by the worker. It was assumed that the "between" groups—the middle classes—would break up. One portion would remain loyal to the established order, but a larger portion under the impact of capitalism itself would go to the ranks and join the workers. The small enterprisers, handicraft workers, et cetera, would be crushed by big business and thus reduced from the middle class to the lower class of wage earner; they would join the revolutionary wage-earner movement. We believed that this would include the small shopkeeper and his kind, but above all, a con-

3

siderable portion of the intellectuals would cast their lot with the proletariat. That was one of the forecasts when I was young, and it was considered a certainty.

Another forecast was that the more advanced countries with more advanced economic systems and technology, such as France, England, and Belgium, would be in the vanguard of revolution. Thirty-five years ago, Germany was considered revolutionary. The German labor movement was looked upon as the model labor movement. For example, if anything were accepted in Germany, Russia followed suit. Russia was happy to take Germany for a model (the German Social Democrats). Russians looked on themselves as junior members of the proletariat. Russia was still in a semibarbaric stage. Agriculture was backward. Russia and the countries east of Russia (China, India) looked to the more advanced countries for leadership, leadership for carrying out the social and political revolution to liquidate capitalism and bring in a socialist or collectivist system.

These principal intellectual landmarks of thirty-five years ago also included the inevitability of war, and here again it was connected with capitalism. War follows the rivalries of capitalistic countries, each endeavoring to set up its own empire. It was taken for granted that capitalism would lead to imperialistic rivalries. British capitalism was able to enhance profits by exploiting British workers, and the market was bound to seek super profits—extraordinary profits outside of Britain—by building up an empire. It was in the empire that Britain put colonial workers to work for little and exploited the consumers—the colonial consumers—and thus British capitalism was able to realize super profits. Since British capitalism aspired to its empire, a clash was inevitable between British and German capitalism. The two systems could not arrive at a stable agreement because their interests clashed. The older capitalism was built first, and the first empire was pushed hard by the new, such as Germany's, so that any peaceful division of the field was, in the long run, impossible. War was inevitable. On the other hand, war was looked on as a splendid opportunity for the proletariat—for the revolutionary proletariat. A defeated country was ripe for revolution. Even a victorious country was so exhausted by war that the conservative elements lost their grip on the situation, and world revolution would emerge as a consequence of imperialistic war. It was taken for granted that the proletariat would be faithful to the revolutionary idea in all countries. There might be some lag between war and revolution, but no one doubted that labor movements, especially the German labor movement, would do the job. That was the forecast of things to come.

Then came the First World War, which supplied us with the first jolt. The labor movements of the warring countries were far from embracing war, but they aligned themselves on the side of their respective governments. The *first shock* was the phenomenon of nationalism—the strength of nationalism among the working people. This was especially so in the most advanced countries, and in the advanced countries is where one depends for revolution. However, these countries decided to follow their governments.

Revolutionaries like Lenin explained the phenomenon on the ground of treason—treason by the leaders. The average workingman was revolutionary, but the leaders flunked out. It was treason at the top. You account for it by saying that imperialism manages to throw a few crumbs to the leadership of the labor movement; these leaders get positions in government. The upper crust—the skilled workers—get concessions; the labor aristocracy, therefore, forgets. The revolution was therefore delayed. It was only a matter of time before there would be a betrayal of the leader and of the upper crust. The proletariat of the more advanced countries of France and England behaved like nationalists, especially the trade unions. They showed themselves to be under the influence of nationalism and their own interests: interests such as membership and conditions of life.

Another shock. While the economically advanced countries flunked out as revolutionary countries, by contrast the proletariat of one backward country—Russia—became the main actor. The German proletariat flunked out, and the small proletariat in Russia (3 or 4 percent of the total population) suddenly came forth and put over a radical revolution. They took possession of the government of the country and became the nucleus of *world-wide revolution.* In 1919 the Third International was established.

The world looked topsy-turvy compared to the system or ideas of certainties. It was surprising and astounding. The explanation given at the time by revolutionary intellectuals was that the proletariat in the more advanced countries showed signs of corruption, but the Russian proletariat was pure and unspoiled and not corrupted by crumbs thrown to it—by concessions and high wages.

The treason and corruption of the leadership and the upper crust of the advanced countries were contrasted with the purity of the Russian proletariat and were considered adequate explanation. With it went a program of purification; the Russian proletariat would purify. It was to constitute the leadership of the world proletariat. The Third International was to be a great movement of purification. It was to replace corrupt leadership and abolish corruption through tutelage; hence, purity-enforcing supervision. That was the program of the Russian Revolution and also the world-wide program. It was to bring on world revolution. Western society was more ready than the Russian society, but it needed more forceful tutelage. It was learned, after awhile, that this was not an easily realized task. Western capitalism—even with the Russian Communists—was hard to dislodge. It was not ripe for liquidation. It was deeply entrenched. The middle classes offered vital support to capitalism, and so did a considerable section of organized labor—trade unionism. It acted as a pylon to the established order. Doubt was cast on the whole basic analysis that capitalism prepares its own grave. Capitalism, once set up, manages to survive. But the revolutionaries never admitted that idea. They said that capitalism is strong, but in another economic crisis it would be so weakened that the proletariat would find its destruction no great task. Another crisis would pull out the capitalist anchor and the proletariat would give the ship a push in the desired direction. So then the hope was that a new and great economic crisis would do the job. In the meantime, the capitalistic countries were drifting farther and farther from a revolutionary program, especially the United States, where there was Coolidge prosperity. The American labor movement in the 1920s was shrinking.

At last a crisis came—in 1929—and it was followed by a prolonged depression which lasted until the capitalistic system was unable to crawl out of the ditch without rearmament and war. The crisis came and it was especially hard on Germany. With the crisis there should have been a revival of the proletariat movement and social revolution. A social revolution did come—but it was vastly different from the one expected. The beneficiaries of the crisis were not the proletariat, or the Communist as he called himself, but the Nazis and Fascists that sprang from the middle-class groups. There was a revolution, but the revolution was not oriented to Communism. The middle classes played an important role. It had been thought that the middle class would not count; that it would have a secondary role—an auxiliary to the established order. But we found in Nazi Germany a plebeian leadership within the lower middle-class groups—people who were social nobodies. They became leaders and took over the churches, parties, government, trade unions, et cetera. I again found that the certainties of my youth had turned out badly. I had thought the middle classes would not count. In 1933 and 1934 I found that the middle classes do play an important part. They have thrust up a leadership and it has proceeded to organize itself as a military and political formation—a phalanx—thrust out by the middle class. The middle-class point of view is represented. Storm troops, secret police, and the like take possession of the nation and then reach out to take the world.

The expectations of thirty-five years ago did not become realized. More recently I have found other surprises. Churchill is the leader of England now,[1] and he is from the aristocracy. In reason, he should stand for the established order. When Hitler attacked Russia last June, Churchill came out and backed Russia. Hitler thought that Churchill would acclaim him. A showdown came when the capitalistic democracies had a chance to snuff out Russia and did not take it. There was enough talk to raise skepticism.

1. Winston Churchill was the Prime Minister of England in 1942.

PART TWO
The Marxist Theory of History

LECTURE 2
The Materialistic Conception of History

A good portion of the semester is given to the exposition of the Marxian system of thought—the *Manifesto*—and continues with commentary. Also Lenin's *State and Revolution.* Your part is to understand, clarify, and expound the thought, that is, concepts and issues raised by Marx. To be able to grasp the whole Marxian system of thought is indispensable.

MARXIAN THEORY OF HISTORY

The theory is called the materialistic conception of history. As a theory of history, what does it exclude? It excludes the conception of a series of accidents of history. The implication is that history is subject to law; the events of history are not just accidental but subject to an underlying law. Another implication is that history is predictable—you can predict what is going to happen—not as in astronomy, but you can predict. History becomes a science, a law of development of human society. Once you have such a formulation, then you are armed with the power of forecasting events. Not at present, but you have the capacity to forecast the future development of order and institutions. Marxism stressed history as a science that can formulate objective laws and predict what will happen in the future. Accidents are ruled out. History is a connected web. In the search for basic laws in historical change, Marxism directs its attention to the sphere of life it considers fundamental— *the activity of making a living.* It is a fundamental activity. Basic in this activity is man's mastery over nature. Marxism calls it *productive forces.* In any period in human history one must make a living, and basic to that are the productive forces.

7

In concrete terms, under the productive forces one would list manual skills and technical knowledge. In agricultural pursuits, technical knowledge is primitive but there is still a storehouse of technical knowledge and skill. In more advanced countries the storehouse is bigger—the tools of production and later machinery. PRODUCTIVE FORCES: (1) *skills*, (2) *technical knowledge*, (3) *tools*, (4) *division of labor*, (5) *machinery*, and (6) *science of management*.

Go into a modern plant and you see that everything is synchronized in order to avoid waste motion. There is a distinct human array—humans are organized in a relationship of command and obedience. It is a productive force and according to the Marxist term, productive forces. The term productive forces covers everything from primitive society to today.

Now for the concept of PRODUCTION RELATIONS. If you visit a plant (such as Ford), you will find a particular kind of human array: some men issue orders (the executives), others carry them out. It is the basis of productive relations. What is the relationship among people engaged in productive practices? At an earlier stage in the development of economic society it was simpler. In the medieval town, production took place in small shops presided over by the workmen's master. One man issued orders and others carried them out—it was a simpler organization. Also in the manorial system, the bailiff was in charge of production and issued orders to the peasants.

Production is carried on by humans who stand in a defined relationship to each other and operate the productive forces. They apply skills and knowledge and use tools and machinery.

So far, I have described the technological situation. Also in production relations we find present the factor of *ownership*. The power to issue commands in production is usually associated with ownership. Ownership is enforced by the government, by government-enforced power. In the medieval manor, the lord owned; and for a long time, while the lord owned the land he owned the peasants. In England serfdom passed away in the fourteenth century. The lord owned the manor and he could issue commands and appoint someone to issue commands. In the medieval city, the master was the owner and he issued commands to the journeyman. The master's ownership of the shop is the basis of his power to issue commands.

In ascending from productive forces to productive relations, we have already brought in, from necessity, the element of property and ownership. In Russia there is no private ownership—it is public and the government owns the plants and appoints management. However, even in Russia there are basic production relations—management and labor—and they are accompanied by the factor of ownership. Of necessity the factor of ownership is brought into production relations, which gives form to production relations.

In the productive process there is a *functional differentiation* as well as a *legalistic differentiation*. The functional refers to those who carry out orders;

and the legalistic is a matter of ownership. These have a distinct differentiation amongst those who take part in production. Functional and legalistic differentiation constitutes the basis of economic classes. In a manorial society, the lords and the serfs were of two economic classes, each representing a functional and a legal differentiation. In modern society the capitalist and the wage earner represent a functional and legal differentiation. In the classical capitalistic set-up there was no such divorce. The capitalist class is a group of people functionally and legally differentiated from the rest. They give orders and own. The proletariat is functionally and legally differentiated too.

Society is divided into economic classes, and the line of division stems from production—the productive process. Class formation stems from the productive process. *Functional and legalistic differentiation is the basis of class formation.*

SOCIETY INTO CLASSES

Marxism says there was a time when society was not separated into classes—was a primitive tribal organization. Marxism insists that society is a picture of different classes stemming from the productive process and relations. And at any given time in the history of a nation one class rules and the others are subject. A ruling class and subject classes. The ruling class manages production in its own interests.

In order to rule within the productive process the ruling class appropriates and controls the vital social institutions and controls them in its own interest. The most vital of all is the government or the state. The control of the government is of importance because the government monopoly controls the physical force. In a class society, it is necessary that the ruling class have a monopoly of physical force. Government is of the greatest importance.

Law, courts of law, principles of property. The ruling class sees to it that courts represent the interests of the ruling class. Courts enforce and recognize the absolute principle of private property. They do not recognize a wage earner's right of property in a job. In a feudal society the courts hold that the rights of law are supreme; the peasant is a tenant of will.

The ruling class really constructs government to serve its own purposes and controls justice. It also controls the educational system, the church, schools, and other agencies that mold opinion, the purpose being to shape the feelings and thoughts of the subject classes into accepting established things. That is the picture of society in a given time that Marxist theory offers us.

All institutions are designed to strengthen the ruling class in its possession of power. And how, according to Marxist theory, does the ruling class achieve its position? The theory is that the position of the ruling class comes not from violence but because it has passed an examination of fitness; that is, its ability to operate in a technological society most efficiently. In the nineteenth century factory owners were the ruling class because they knew what no one else knew. They had the fitness to operate modern industry. They had grown up with it and developed it.

The ruling class comes to power not by accident or by pulling wires, but because at that time it can best discharge the social function. The ruling class rises because of its fitness and it takes the place of the class that has lost its fitness. In the Middle Ages, the feudal nobility was fit to rule. It could operate a simple technological society. It could fight and protect the serfs. Then there were changes in industry—inventions, skills, and the like. In the new environment the lords were nonplussed and they lost their managerial fitness. They lost the productive process in life and got out of it. They hung on because they wanted to rule, and they had to be dislodged by a revolution; a new class and the only one fit to rule was the bourgeoisie. The mass followed the capitalist class. They could offer a more effective economic life—a higher standard of living. People supported the bourgeoisie (the capitalistic class). The capitalist class being a productive class fit to manage came forth and displaced the old class that had become parasitic.

LIFE CYCLE OF THE ECONOMIC CLASS—CAPITALIST CLASS

The capitalist class started in the medieval cities on a small scale and for a number of years and centuries even conducted itself modestly. Its members bowed to the king and church, but they were developing something new— modern business—producing for a larger market. They benefited from inventions. By and by, within society there grew cells of a new society: the society of business. Slowly this new class of businessmen threw off their modesty. They no longer felt low and became class conscious and felt that a greater role was yet to come. They united people against the established order of things. They put it over successfully. They fought it out in the political arena and destroyed things characteristic of the feudal nobility, replacing them with institutions of their own—namely, a democratic form of government. They abolished the privileges of the church and took over the courts. They expelled or liquidated the old ruling class and put themselves in their place. They were acclaimed by the people and made it possible for the productive forces to render more to society. After they had established themselves as the ruling class they unleashed productive forces. Then there was a tremendous Industrial Revolution—a world market, et cetera. Here is the progressive portion of the life cycle of the bourgeois class: victory and rulership and then a period of productivity. They were at their zenith of functional fitness and by and by they passed their zenith. Institutions began to operate as a straitjacket for productive forces and it was seen that periodic depressions occurred. People were out of work and plants were idle.

LECTURE 3
The Life Cycle of the Ruling Class

Last time I discussed the materialistic conception of history. It wove around the concepts of (1) productive forces–skill, technical knowledge, tools, machinery, scientific management–and (2) production relations–the human array–those that manage and those that carry out orders. They handle productive forces. Next, already in the concept of production relations you have more than a trace of the concept of property; usually those who issue commands own. In medieval times the lord owned the manor. Later on came cities and the beginnings of industry. Ownership conferred the power to manage, to issue commands, to hold a commanding position. Emphasis is thrown upon the productive process. There is functional differentiation among humans in the process. Functional differentiation results in distinct classes. A ruling class and a subject class or classes result; the concept of an economic class and ruling class. The ruling class does not arrive at rulership by accident or by exercise of physical force or by wire pulling. It becomes the ruling class by virtue of its fitness at the time to administer and operate the productive forces of society. It gives productive forces room for development. The ruling class is the result of functional differentiation.

The period in question–the class capable of passing a higher exam than other classes as regards efficient administration of productive forces in society– that is how the capitalistic class came to replace feudal nobility. Capitalists developed business and industry, and new productive forces were confined under the feudal regime–so the capitalist class appears as the releaser of productive forces held in check by the earlier regime. ("Regime" refers to the organization of government.)

The most important attribute of a ruling class is that it controls government. Government is its tool–it looks after its interest. The ruling class, an economic class, arrives at its post by virtue of fitness. There is the belief that it is critical that the ruling class dominate institutions, especially government, because government is the wielder of physical force and keeps subject classes in line. The ruling class must control the government. It also controls the courts, legal principles, and especially, the law of property–these as well as the spiritual institutions of society, the church, education, artistic life, and so on. These are managed and shaped in accord with the ruling class; thus there is a class society presided over by the ruling class that arises as a result of functional differentiation in the productive process. It has the ability to administer. The ruling class passes an efficiency test, but before establishing itself as ruler, it must capture the government. That means pushing the old government off the boards. Having seized political power—government—the ruling class reshapes other institutions. The Marxist concept of government—the shape of government—is unique to a particular period in history. Each ruling class builds up its own mechanism of government. First, it must destroy the old mechanism of government and replace it with one adapted to its own interests. When a class comes to power it does not take over the old government, but smashes it and builds up a new one. Government is a particular tool. Each ruling class, when it arrives at power, must build up a structure of its own and that means revolution. Revolution involves two things: (1) pushing the old government out and (2) building up a new government mechanism. In feudal times it was a government of estates (fixed), but when the capitalistic class appeared the government was smashed and replaced by a capitalistic democracy. The capitalistic class was not afraid to give suffrage because, when it was first in power, it really represented the interests of the masses of people. The capitalist class was best fitted to improve the standard of living of all the people. All groups were to benefit from the change in the ruling class.

LIFE CYCLE OF A RULING CLASS

The ruling class in the cradle—the capitalistic class—it started in the medieval towns. Towns were weak affairs and surrounded by hostile feudal bands. The capitalistic class had to be modest and use the friction among the feudal lords as well as with the king. Masters and traders had to lie low, but they were enhancing their economic importance. Still, they were doing so without putting forth any demands. The time came when they saw themselves as being important and powerful and doing something for society, namely, managing industry and trade. They became class conscious. They began to say, "We are the salt of the earth! We keep society going." That meant they saw themselves as destined for a great role, and they put forward their candidacy to be the ruling class. They had the people on their side because they were progressive. The Marxist interpretation of a progressive class does not mean a class that has all the moral virtues, but one that can administer productive forces efficiently and does not hold them back. It furthers the development of productive forces.

   The life cycle reaches a point where the group is class conscious, progressive, and furthers the development of productive forces and is not afraid to be the champion of the people. It is the leader of the masses. With the aid of the masses it upsets the old ruling class and comes to power, continuing in a progressive phase. Productive forces are given their head and race forward; there is a rapid development in production. For a while there is harmony. The old ruling class rarely accepts defeat, however, and watches for a chance to come back. The new ruling class has a police organization to watch, but as yet it is not attacked by the masses because they are still content with the change. The capitalistic class, due to its progressive role, is willing to give the masses more education and a formal share in the government—the ballot. The only menace is from the right, the past—the old ruling class.

So far, I am depicting the ruling class in a stage of vigor—its youth. It is unafraid and looking to the future with confidence. It is progressive in several senses. It furthers productive forces, and in a political sense the progressive worker casts a ballot. Nature controls. Then the institutions that the new ruling class established begin to be hindrances to the development of the productive forces.

In this life cycle, 1857 was a turning point. In this year there was a world-wide economic crisis—the first world-wide economic depression. It is the first symptom that the capitalistic class is losing its fitness. It was fit yesterday because it was progressive. Now something has changed that is analogous to one's discovery, when he is in his forties or fifties, that he can't climb hills. No longer is the capitalistic class progressive. It is lost so far as being able to further the productive forces, and it is also lost politically. No longer is it free and easy in giving political rights to the masses—it is afraid of them. It sees in the workers not an auxiliary to maintain its own rule, but enemies and potential enemies. In our depicting of the life cycle of the ruling class, we are now following a downward curve. The class is losing its confidence that it can master any situation, and economic depressions are an external manifestation of its fear.

Structural changes in society. The middle-class groups were formerly a mainstay of capitalism; now they melt away. Big business grinds down the middle class. The social foundation on which capitalism existed begins to crack. Labor rises in numbers and grows in power. Labor becomes class conscious under the impact of the standard of living and the life—at first in a timid way by strikes, later on with the aid of intellectuals and certain members of the upper class, who will rebel against their own class and come over to the wage earners and find out what it is all about. They will think of themselves as playing a role. This was emphasized by Marx himself in 1864 when he organized the First International organization in London. He wanted to win over the British Trade Unionists, to persuade them to come into the International and so, in his inaugural address of 1864, he expressed the purposes of the organization. In his address he also depicted the role that labor was going to play in reshaping society. Marx was a middle-class intellectual who wanted to educate labor and make it feel class conscious. So he went out of his way to tell the laborers how important they already were and he gave them credit for things that could not really be credited to them, such as the ten-hour day and labor laws concerning women and children. The leaders in these things were conservative reformers. Marx told the British about their role—what a great role they were already playing in society. He told them that what is needed is science for the working class. The term "science" was vague and purposely so. Marx meant social science, and that was Marxism—the science of social revolution. The role played by the intellectuals was to serve as awakeners of labor, which they saw as destined to be the new ruling class.

His talk was muffled because he did not want to scare British labor. He told them about the union of science in the working class which would bring about real democracy.

In 1871 there was a revolt in Paris and the setting up of the Commune of Paris. Marx chose to interpret this revolt as the first attempt at revolution of the proletariat. There were all sorts of things involved: the Parisians did not want to be governed by the provinces; the shopkeepers were discontented; and so on. This resulted in an explosion. But to Marx it proved the proletariat baby was coming along fine. After three months, the Commune was liquidated, but it was only a temporary defeat. Marx still believed the proletariat had it in it to be a ruling class. He pounced on the Commune as his child: it was proof to him that the proletariat had it in it to assume the urgently needed role of commandant of the future. That meant the bourgeoisie would go the way of feudalism and that meant a new type of government—the first political revolution and a new government structure. Just as the capitalists destroyed the old feudal state, so the proletariat destroyed the capitalists in 1871, according to Lenin. The proletariat showed through its own political constructiveness what kind of political structure was its own. From what the Commune of Paris did, Lenin deduced his Soviet System.

Here is *the life cycle of a ruling class*—the capitalistic class illustration. Cradle —the guild system when the capitalist pleads to exist as a small craftsman. Then follows a period of greatness of the class and they shove out the feudal nobility. Then the class goes downward; it loses progressiveness and is eventually liquidated by the new ruling class, the proletariat, which starts from its own social cradle and is weak, cutting loose under the instruction of science. The Marxist proletariat rises in might and puts an end to the preceding ruling class. That is the life cycle of the ruling class. The ruling class starts from the productive process as a result of functional differentiation.

Hordes of invaders from Asia conquered the Byzantine Empire, Europe, China, et cetera, but were just conquerors—good fighters who developed a new type of maneuvering on horses. From an economic standpoint they represented an inferior society. The Mongols knew little of production; they were nomads. The conquered countries possessed more advanced economic development. In general, in the Marxist scheme, these empires of nomad origin—merely flashes in the pan—did not last long. They were not in the mainstream of history. The mainstream of history in pattern—power in government, power over society— stemmed from the economic function, the ability to administer—the Marxist concept of power formation.[1] Marx's concept is that *power stems from economic function.* Only if you grant that power stems from the ability to administer productive forces, only then can you speak of a definite law of history. The Marxist theory of power: the economic class or social class that has power in the first phase of life is an economic functioning class.

LECTURE 4
The Class Struggle and Rival Conceptions of History

The materialistic conception of history is an attempt to formulate a science of history, a law of motion of society. It is an ambitious undertaking to introduce science into human affairs. This excludes the concept of history as a mere string of accidents. Accidents are just accidents—they are not caused. To make a science of anything, you have to point out the causality—the cause and effect relationships. One must formulate causality between events. The next step in formulating causality is singling out the elements. In chemistry the way to explain chemical compounds is first to formulate elements and show, as to quality and quantity, what is present in a compound.

The Marxist concept of history endeavoring to be a science proceeded to designate the history-making elements—classes. History is a class struggle, a record of class struggles. History is not made by such things as the ambition of kings, but by the struggling classes. Individuals may strut on the historical arena but they are held by strings. Strings proceed from the class struggle. The struggles of classes—that is the basic historic process. The historical process stripped of superficialities is a struggle between classes.

Another thing—what are the classes struggling for? what controls the struggle? Classes struggle for power and their struggle is not controlled or caused by the will of God. The biblical interpretation of the flow of events is ruled out. The Divine Will and individual will is out of it. What is in, is the self-interested and self-centered behavior of social classes. Social classes are not just social but economic classes. There is the struggle of economic classes.

The origin of classes. They originate in the productive process, that is, in the

---

1. See Lectures 6 and 7 for an elaboration on the idea of power, particularly its organization.

handling of productive forces; they spring from the functional differentiation. Functional differentiation—production relations, Marx called it.

Economic classes stem from functional differentiation in the productive process, in the handling of productive forces. What are productive forces? They are human and extrahuman. The human mind is a storehouse of past information, technical knowledge and skill, also future skill. Human and extrahuman, but mostly human. Marx says there is a gradual and unrelenting accumulation of productive forces, the store of human technical knowledge. This is the basic process, and this theory assumes that humans progress and improve technical knowledge. The human is a tool-making animal. Productive forces are a process of invention and addition to the technical storehouse of knowledge. It is as inevitable as the movement of a glacier. What determines the tempo of the accumulation of productive forces? Growth? It is influenced by the human institutions. Sometimes they favor accretion of forces and sometimes they hinder. So you have feudal institutions or proletariat institutions, capitalist institutions, and on down the line. One wants to impose human institutions on all human society—social institutions, especially government and law. (Government is important—the law of property especially.) So under feudal institutions you had property that was physical and there was human property too. The law of the manor supervises the productive process. Later on, under the capitalist set of institutions, the human buys and sells his human labor and the law of property favors the capitalist, the owner of property. Government, law, and especially the law of property—these are the most important elements and a ruling class must control them in order to rule.

Institutions may at one time further encourage these forces or hinder them. but it was influenced by money—a law of property that favored capitalists. But when it was first put in, it was a distinct improvement over what had preceded it. Under capitalism the worker is a free man. In the feudal system men were serfs and enterprise was shackled. Under the feudal system business was hindered and factories were not rising as fast as they might. When the capitalistic system was in government it became friendly to business and furthered it. Business could benefit from limited liability and invest; it was safe to go afield. Particular social institutions reflecting the interest of a class can further or hinder the growth of productive forces. When a class furthers them, it is said to be in its productive phase. The productive forces are tribunal. They sit in judgment upon the ruling classes of the time and upon the institutions. During the first phase of the life cycle or at its zenith people say the institutions of a class are fine. Institutionalization is fine. After awhile the productive forces are not so good for the ruling class as is institutionalization. By and by things go wrong. You have depressions, and they arise because there is no plan of production under capitalism. As a result there is a lot of disjointedness also. Or, as Marxists say, an anarchy of production results in disjointedness (anarchy equals nongovernment). Some industries are out of joint with other industries.

Private profit is the sole incentive of production, and that means exploitation. Exploitation is depriving the wage earner of the full wage for what he produces. If capitalists' profits come from appropriating part of the value of the worker and the worker cannot buy back, the result is a depression. A Marxist says the productive forces are rising in rebellion. Private profit-making: formerly the institutions of capitalism made room for the productive forces but now the productive forces are cramped and cannot expand. Half of the industries are closed and the productive forces have a scowl on their faces and say this cannot last much longer; sooner or later the house will burst asunder; we are cramped for space. The house collapses and the productive forces are now in a new mansion built by the proletariat class. It had developed under capitalism. Now the proletariat takes over and rules. A social revolution has occurred and the institutions of capitalism are all smashed. The smashing is done by human hands and those of the proletariat. There is a proletariat state as well as law and universities. The productive forces are now satisfied that they have been released from the straitjacket. Here there is more than a touch of wishful thinking. The happy ending is when the proletariat wins and builds a mansion. It is a magic mansion; its walls will stretch when the productive forces grow. Planning and inventions will be put to use and the productive forces will grow and no longer need a wing of the institutional mansion, because the mansion will expand. It will be so magical because it is a planned society—everything is planned. This is the scheme or skeleton of the materialistic conception of history. It is called the materialistic conception because of cause and effect in history pertaining to the material interests of humanity—to the interests of survival. The economic use of resources—the process of making a living, caring for the material interests—*there* is where the engine of history is hidden. Where the productive process carries on, there is where the engine is housed.

A rival conception of history. After you have rejected the view that history is just an accident, you don't have to come to the materialistic concept necessarily. You might come to (1) *the theological concept of history*: the best illustration of that is the book of the Bible. The Book of Joshua in the Bible is a historical document. The Bible was written by the Jews and they were a historical people—and a self-centered people—who told stories about themselves. The major part of the Bible refers to the history of a small people. In the Books of Joshua and Exodus, the people were brought out of Egypt; Moses brought them to the promised land. There they conquered tribes and settled. They misbehaved and continued to do so and they were great repenters. And when they misbehaved (fell away from the commandments of the law), then the Lord sent a foreign conqueror who enslaved them. Then they repented and thought of the commandments and returned to the law. Then a leader arose and prepared a rebellion against the foreign oppression. But they never stayed put that way. Again they sinned. You can call that an interpreta-

tion of history. Moderns say that the book is an early chronicle that did not
philosophize, a chronicle edited by one of the priestly class who interpreted
these events. Interpretation was inserted. That gives you a unified theory of
unification. It is a theological interpretation.

Other interpretations: (2) *the ethical interpretation.* This is an interpretation
that says God or Nature has inserted in the human being a propensity to work
for justice, or for what is fair. Human history is an unfolding of humans striving
for relationships. First as a small group, and as time goes on, the craving for
justice becomes more intense and embraces mankind. That is the official philosophy of modern democracies. In the democratic way of life the human is treated as an end in himself. A person brings out all the potentialities in himself—
fairness, the desire to be and have good neighbors, and the like. The ethical
interpretation often speaks of God. Humans have God and that makes them
different from animals. But you can omit God and stress that Nature is beneficent. Nature, whether divine molding or inherent in self, was beneficent, and
when we, as humans, live we discover something in us to urge us to realize
greater freedom. This is an ethical interpretation. You cannot speak of the
main force of history-making but as pulling from in front—the urge to realize
an *ethical* idea. The desire to realize human ideals comes either from God or
is implanted by Nature. Ideals found expression in Christianity or democracy.

(3) *The political interpretation.* Here the Germans excel. Schmoller had a
theory of history. To him the driving force in history was the political ruler,
or the monarch. He used this interpretation in his own Prussia where the land
was poor and sandy, with only pine trees. Out of an unpromising beginning
under leaders or monarchs—later the kings of Prussia—modern Germany arose.
The unifying factor is the state, the government. First the chief and then the
king who became the chief. The emphasis is on the political factor, not on
economic classes but on the visible government—officials taking orders from
kings. It assumes that there are groups who are walking appendages, who cannot do anything by themselves. They prevent economic progress. Before the
coming of the authoritative intervention of the king of Prussia you had many
selfish towns and cities each looking after its own interests. They treated neighbors as foreigners and gave them no cooperation. If towns and estates had been
permitted to go on in their own way, there would have been stagnation. But
the monarch came and he forced the towns to give up their selfishness. He first
used coercion and rammed prosperity down their throats. He made a great
nation. Later on it was the nucleus of Germany. That was the German empire.

PART THREE
Politics of the Marxist Theory of State and Revolution

LECTURE 5
The Ethics and Structure of Government

The materialistic conception, or theory, of history: stress is laid upon the material conditions of life, the productive process, the economic classes shaping history and the ruling class shaping institutions.

Ethics—is there room for ethics? Unselfish behavior—is it possible under Marx's theory of history? Have we all been gangsters or egotists? Is there room for idealism—unselfish action—in the Marxist theory? The answer is yes. In the Marxist concept of history there is room for idealism. It does not deny the ethical impulse in man. It says the ethical impulse in man is taken in hand by the material conditions of life, which makes you class conscious. If you are a member of a particular class, you will make sacrifices for that particular class and identify the humanitarian with that class. You may have pure ideals, but the stuff out of which ideals are made is thrown at you by the interest of the class. Thus there is no such thing as abstract ethics or universal ethics. An ethical system is always shaped by the interest of the class. Marx stresses the ethical propensity, or impulse, in man. The ideal comes not from heaven but is shaped by the interests of the particular class to which you belong. The materialistic concept of history gives you material ideals. (The idealist is not determined by material things of life.) The ideal is a historical product and arises out of the class you identify yourself with. While sacrificing, you are not aware of the class idea.

In the Marxist concept of history there is plenty of room for heroic, ideal action—self-sacrificing action. The ideal itself is materialistically shaped. It reflects the class that a person belongs to.

19

SELF-IDENTIFICATION WITH A PARTICULAR CLASS

Not all individuals identify themselves with the class they are born into or with. Some are for the rightists; they may turn traitors to their own class, because they realize their class is no longer vigorous and they leave the ruling class. These intellectuals choose to alter their allegiance and declare it to the lower classes that have a future. Not only do they alter allegiance, but they themselves may serve as awakeners of class consciousness of a new rising class. They are history's alarm clocks—alarm clocks from the old ruling class—and they shake the new class out of its slumbers and teach it. Individuals may identify themselves with classes not their own.

STATE OR GOVERNMENT

What is government in the Marxist system of thought? Some people say government is an agency that carries out common interest. Marxism identifies government with the ruling class of the particular time. *It is the executive committee of the ruling class of the particular society.* In our own day, rule was from the feudal nobility to the industrialist. Then we say government is the executive committee of the capitalist class. It was said to be democracy in form only; in substance government is the tool of the capitalist class. The democratic form of government did not yield a government that is the common agent of all, but it existed as the executive committee of the capitalistic class. Government is not something serving the general social interest. But government under all circumstances is the tool of the ruling class and keeps the class in power, protects property interests, and so forth. Government is a tool whose prime purpose is to perpetuate the ruling class and protect the ruling class.

THE STRUCTURE OF GOVERNMENT OR INSTRUMENTALITIES

The army, police force, judicial apparatus, and the like constitute bureaucracy—official government. These are the instrumentalities. It is Marx's idea that the instrumentalities of government are not merely neutral tools like an axe that one can use to chop down trees and build a house—or use to commit a murder. (The axe is a neutral tool.) Some say that government is a neutral tool, like the army, which protects the interests of one class and shoots when power shifts from one class to another.

There are two theories of government: the theory of constitutional evolution and the theory of revolution. The evolutionary theory is that one class succeeds another and takes over the instruments of government. The capitalist class brought in democracy and there was an electorate. The electorate exists geographically as a constituency. The government is elected by votes of the people and voting units are geographic units; so people say why couldn't the proletariat make use of the same thing? By electioneering they could take over the majority and the existing agents of government, merely appointing new ministers of a new class. That is not the Marxist theory; it is the evolution theory.

Marx's theory says it cannot be done. Each class, when it rules, must smash the government and the political life that formerly existed, smash the old form of political organization and old instrumentalities. It must be built from the ground up, both as to form and personnel. The new state is based on *occupational units,* and the capitalist is denied the right to vote. Only working people vote, and they vote by factories, plants, and productive units. A hierarchy, consisting of councils, or soviets, and topped by the national soviet, composes its structure. All the way through there is an exclusion of the old ruling class from any participation in political life. So you then have a new form of political life, presumably fitting the proletariat.

The democratic form must not be taken over, because it will play a dirty trick if it is. The old ruling class will steal the government. Thus, alter the government and deny the old ruling class any right in the government. New instrumentalities must be built—the old army cannot be used. Build up a new one with officers from the working classes—a proletarian army. Abolish old courts and get new judges from among the working people. Also disband the old bureaucracy and create a new one. These new official groups—the bureaucracy—will remain close to the people, Lenin thought. And be sure they do so and that they are not paid any more than the working man. *That is the Marxian concept of state and revolution.*

There is no possibility for a peaceful transition. No ruling class voluntarily gives up its power. The only way to get rid of it is to defeat it and smash it. There were two exceptions that Marx made—two countries that might go to the proletariat without a revolution—England and the United States, because there were no standing armies. The ruling class is in no position to crush the proletariat when it makes demands. England is a naval power, and this is no good. If there is no standing army the ruling class is incapable of crushing the power of the proletariat. The same holds true if there is no bureaucracy—which England did not have until the nineteenth century. Government was by prestige. The landed gentry ruled in particular localities; they had judicial functions but no pay. Thus there was no large bureaucratic class.

The United States might escape bloody revolution, too, because the ruling class has no effective agents of oppression, such as a large standing army and a bureaucracy.

Aside from these exceptions, Marx was clear: no ruling class would give up voluntarily, because they have an army, police, and the like and use them. Thus you cannot avoid bloody revolution. There is no peaceful transition. He used the French Revolution as an example of the shift of rule from one to another. The French nobility fought and called in foreign governments to put down the Revolution, and their leaders plotted to ruin the new government. Many left and joined the armies of the invading nations to crush the Revolution. There is no possibility of effecting a peaceful transition from one regime to another except in the United States and England.

You cannot rely upon the established hierarchies. The army is constructed in such a way that it only serves the capitalistic class. You cannot take over the army to serve the purpose of the new class. The army is built on subordination; the officer is a god, the soldiers merely mud on boots. (In the proletariat army, the officer is not put on a pedestal; an officer is just a commander.) Officers have ideas of elite, so you have to have a new army, a Red army. The same holds true for the judiciary and bureaucracy. That is Marx's and Lenin's concept of state and revolution.

SIDE OBSERVATIONS

Another theory of government is that government *does not bind itself to organized economic groups.* Society is divided into groups, and economic lines of division are important. So you have economic classes out to benefit themselves. The business class, workingmen in unions, and farmers in associations—the organized groups—do not insist that the unit of government be individual, but these groups follow economic lines. Where does the government figure? It is a government manned by politicians. There are two political concerns: the Republican party and the Democratic party. Each is out to get from the electorate on election day a contract to govern. There is a free election—reasonably free. The electorate decides between two rival concerns, each bidding to contract to govern. Each names a price, what it will do if it gets the contract. These are two political concerns who make a business of government and they are out to contract government jobs—Congress, jobs in Washington and elsewhere. Each of the two concerns is composed of individuals of varied qualifications—silk hats (pure) and ward heelers. The two political concerns are composed of politicians of various grade or caliber with varying codes of ethics. These political concerns are quite cognizant of the existing groups, such as farmers and teachers, and would like to get votes. A bargaining process results. There is collective bargaining in politics. Labor organizations approach one party and then the other to see what is offered to them; then they decide how to vote. This is the picture of American life today. *How does it fit in the Marxist picture?*

It calls the two parties capitalistic parties. They are not different and both are capitalistic. Marx says, from the standpoint of the proletariat there is nothing to choose, so do away with both. The American workingman never listened to Marx, but got himself mixed up with politics. They make bargains or exercise pressure politics.

The government in office—what is it? It is just government. It is subject to pressure. There is little difference in one kind of government or another. One is more sympathetic to labor than the other, just different by degree. That is the picture of American political life, and it is gaining political influence in America.

The composition of the parties. The Democratic party—what would you call it in a social analysis? The Democratic party is a peculiar aggregate. The solid South is conservative; it is anti labor legislation. The South is solidly Democratic. Chicago, with its Kelly-Nash machine,[1] is in politics for what it can get, and there is a buildup of political machines. If you get the unemployed jobs, they are grateful for life. The whole process is built on favors. Labor bargained collectively and received a working partnership. Humanitarians are pure idealists. When you have an agglomerate, the question is, Which is the dog and which the tail? Thus there is a need for political artistry. In the last seven years we have had a humanitarian politician; the tail wags the dog.

How do you fit this in with Lenin's and Marx's system? You cannot. In studying American social and political life, you must form your own categories as I did. A political guild and its objective is to win the election. For that reason it is flexible, and if progressivism is in the air it nominates a progressive humanitarian. But somehow the business of government is done.

LECTURE 6
Politics as Seen by Marxism

THE POLITICS OF MARXISM: THE RISE OF POWER AND THE PRESSURES OF POWER FORMATION

Marx's theory is that political power stems from the economically functioning class. The ruling class scores on its efficiency; it operates better than any other class at the time. Then it reaches out for power. Power or the formation of power is conceived of as an economic class becoming class conscious, organizing, and putting forth its claim. When the old is pushed off the board the new

1. Chicago city political machine in the 1930s.

contender comes forth and establishes its own political organization. The Marxist power formation is a sharp incident in the rise of economic classes.

How about national power—the rise of countries as independent powers, like the rise of the United States, the rise of unified Germany as a great power, and the rise of Italy? How does Marxism account for the rise of nationalism? On the face of it, it is not the rise of a particular class but the rise of a whole nation. Marx answers that we must go behind the record. The class struggle knows how to disguise itself in the rise of a nation. The rise of a nation is the substance of nothing else but the rise of a particular class—the capitalists. Austria-Hungary may be viewed as a patriarch. Some of its people resented the domination of the Germans. Marx's interpretation of the Czech struggle was that it was a struggle for independence. Marx says the Czech struggle for national independence was a disguised struggle of the Czech bourgeoisie for (1) a monopoly of the Czech market. The Germans took the market so that the market in the Czech-speaking land was a monopoly of the German bourgeoisie, and that was the monopoly that the Czech capitalist class wanted to break down. The Czech national struggle, according to Marx, was a struggle of the Czech bourgeoisie for the market and (2) a struggle to constitute itself as an independent entity. When it had gained strength as a state, then it could annex foreign markets. Marx said the Czech national struggle, when all Czechs took part, had as its nucleus the bourgeoisie.

The Marxist interpretation: struggles for national independence in the seventeenth century and again in the nineteenth century were not as the record showed, but manifestations of history-making class struggle. National struggles, then, are reduced to class struggles, the struggle of the bourgeoisie of a weak nation in order to gain indispensable allies.

Digression. Criticism of what I am expounding is something of vital import— the struggle of national entities for independence. The German unification, the Italian unification, or China today—manifest struggles for national independence. To some it is a class struggle, but in our historical process it is important in what form the struggle takes place. To me the brightest thing today is the rise of China as a national power. The Marxian interpretation of the Chinese national movement—would it be the Chinese bourgeoisie wanting to get out from under? That is a factor in the situation, no doubt, but it is important in the historic process to have power arise not offensively but defensively—live and let live.

The rise of the United States as a national entity. Class struggle (economic interpretation), a good many Marxists point out, was started in the United States by the merchants. But look at the history-making importance of that factor. In the process there was formulated a great ideology—the right of all nations to throw off the yoke of their oppressor and the duty of the free to help those throwing off the yoke of their masters. The United States aided the Latin American countries. We did not help because of markets but because of ideological sympathy. The United States got independence by warring against foreign masters. England did aid Latin America, but only for the balance of power.

China today. Their phenomenon, I think, will have the same influence on idealism as the thirteen colonies in their independence from England—first, because the Chinese nation was hammered together not by aggression and annexing foreign lands, but it was united by fighting a foreign oppressor. That is why China is the spokesman for India. It is her idealism and it will affect the future.

Contrast this with Germany. Here also, there was an idealistic movement, and it was among the educated and middle-class Germans in the nineteenth century. The movement was sidetracked and captured by Bismarck. The result was that the process of German unification was brought about by iron and blood—unified not by idealism but by aggression and the use of sharp means that denied idealism. The result was an effect on the whole history-making process quite different from the American history-making power, and that of China too.

Italy is an interesting case because Italy also had a strong idealistic national movement under Mazzini. Italy was not unified by its own blood and iron but by other rulers' blood and iron—first by Napoleon III and then by Bismarck. Italian national unification left a mixed and vague imprint on history. On the one hand there was the Mazzini idealism, but on the other hand the trick was done by blood and iron. That is why Italian nationalism was an anemic one. Italian nationalism began in the Turkish War, 1911, and was later continued by Mussolini.

It makes a big difference if you agree with Marx about the interest of class and the bourgeoisie of a country. But as we see, the manner in which national unification takes place does have a tremendous effect upon history. That is why China will arrive at a position of great power. I prophesy that if Germany loses, in future years to come, the weak nations of the world will look to China. China will be the spokesman. China will enjoy the same prestige that America had in the nineteenth century. It will have prestige of honor, independence, and all without violence.

I never insist upon any one factor explaining a complicated situation. Many factors shape a situation. There is class struggle too. Chinese intelligence is asking to do something for the masses, et cetera.

We are witnessing world-shaking events. Not only aggression, but an idealistic process of hammering a nation together.

The politics of Marxism. Of necessity, power formation is of an economic class. That is the proletariat materialistic interpretation of power formation.

Now, let us question that authority. The empire of the Mongols was the greatest that human history saw. It extended from southern China to western Europe in the thirteenth and fourteenth centuries. Who were the Mongols?

The Mongols were west-wing Tartars who conquered and held highly advanced countries, economically and industrially. They did it because the Mongols had a military and political gift. They knew how to fight. They were also skillful governors. They did not care about religious or other institutions. They were just concerned with tribute. They were not producers (of course, they produced, but productive forces at their disposal were meager). In a sense they were gangsters. Their *secret of domination*—sheer physical power, military and political skill.

How does that fit in the Marxist theory of the history of power formation? You cannot say it was a flash in the pan, because it lasted two or three hundred years and continued under the Turks. In our own day we have witnessed internal conquest—military and political skill—in the conquest of Germany by the Nazi party. Who were the Nazis prior to 1933? They were superfluous people for whom there was no room in society. Many were psychotic cases; they were queer. You cannot say they represent the rise to power or that they were the orthodox Marxist formation. The Marxist interpretation had to do a little adjusting, pushing phenomena into its own form. So it said, Never mind the Nazis—they are going places because they can fight, but they are merely henchmen, agents of the embattled capitalistic class. Never mind that on the surface there is physical violence; at the bottom it is finance capital, bankers, and big industrialists of Germany, and they are pulling wires. The explanation was, Do not be misguided by mere appearances—there is someone wiser than Hitler who does the real policy-making, someone in finance capital. Now to those concerned with saving doctrine, this is solace. That was the explanation of the Nazi phenomenon. It is really economic—at the bottom is finance capital—and that makes it all meaningful according to the Marxists.

But if we look at it soberly with no desire to save any theory, the above explanation is not so convincing. Many finance capitalists who thought they could rule under Hitler were disappointed. To be sure, as Hitler climbed to power, he was nice to the capitalists and led them to think they were two-fisted young fellows and would take orders. So the Nazis coaxed the capitalists for funds. Once they reached power, there was a change, but it was not all at once. They had to feel more confident, get their fangs into the politics and the economy. You could argue that Nazis were just henchmen, or you could argue that it was just pretense. It was a transitional period—June 30, 1934, Hitler made a blood purge and killed the more radical Nazis who were against the capitalists. One could say, Look, they killed their own members. But as we look at it now, the thing is far from simple and certainly does not look as if the purge was a triumph of the capitalist group in the Nazi party. If you want to find out who has power and runs things, you will see who makes the most *crucial decisions.* The most crucial is the decision of making war. War today is the life or death stake of a nation. So if you want to find out what group rules a country today, just find out who decides war. The decision to attack Poland was made by the top leadership of the Nazi party (Hitler). The decision to attack Russia was Hitler's.

So the way to understand the Nazi phenomenon is not to cramp it into Marxism. No doubt a considerable segment of capitalists in Germany did bring the Nazis into power and the Junkers helped bring the Nazis into power. The Nazi phenomenon is something like the Mongol phenomenon in the thirteenth and fourteenth centuries—political skill and a certain kind of military skill within the country. The Nazi party excelled in assassinations and political talents. It was not a group of people who excelled in technological development. Some Nazi leaders have become great owners. Goering is a great owner— he took property because he is the leader of the party of physical violence.

LECTURE 7
Political Power

THE RELATION BETWEEN ECONOMIC FITNESS AND POLITICAL POWER

The Marxian theory of the state was the ability to handle productive forces, which led to the gaining of political power.

At the end of the last meeting, I discussed other sources of political power— political power kept not only for a short period but for centuries where the group was not interested in the management of economic life. I mentioned the Mongol conquest. They could manage war and government.

The Turkish rulers never wanted the Turks to become businessmen. They wanted to keep their own people peasants and warriors. Their ambition was to maintain themselves in power as a fighting race. Here you have a phenomenon of political power basing itself on military power.

Another example is the North and South of the United States. Which of the sections manifested the most successful political power? The South—the South ruled the nation prior to the war. The Southern planters belonged to the past in Marxist thought. They looked back. In the North was the industrialist. When it came to political power or military power, the Southern planters—this backward class—stood for a system that was past. The South based itself upon more punitive methods; the North was based on technology. The South had the best of it, however, in politics. However, it was smothered by the greater population of the North. So far as political and military capacity was concerned, the South was superior.

Regarding the present German situation, to my way of thinking the rise of the Nazis shows political power not rising on the basis of economic power but on the basis of organizing a political military movement. In the Nazi phenomenon one can see political power rising independently of the economic function.

I am raising questions. Shouldn't we loosen up our notion of power formation? Must we confine it to economics? Shouldn't we be more liberal and recognize that it springs from all kinds of sources? Sometimes there is high economic proficiency or low.

Why did Marxism trot out the economic class as the one? Maybe because it bore a stamp of its own century—the stamp of the nineteenth century. Marx was a product of the nineteenth century.

What was there about the nineteenth century, especially to Marx, who did not look to the backward parts of Europe but abroad? Marx was a Westerner— to him the hub of civilization was England and France. When he looked to England he saw the rise of an economic group and saw it squeezing out the old ruling class—the Reform bill of 1832. He saw struggling England—the struggle between the landlord class and the industrialists. They put themselves at the head of the popular movement. In the rotten boroughs, one landlord would send several members to Parliament. But now industrialists were coming up from the cities. Marx saw in England the rise of an economic group that spread from technology. Robert Owen was a representative from the manufacturing class. Marx saw the rise to political power of an economic class, and when he looked again at England, he saw a similar struggle in the lower ranks of the people—in a good many workers. They were organizing a political movement called the Chartist movement. They demanded a charter, six points all aimed at more democratic government. In the eyes of Marx they were the working people. When Marx looked at the most advanced country of the world it was England. In the second quarter of the nineteenth century the political arena had three contenders, and each an economic class. The landlords prior to 1832 had control of everything. They had rent. They stood for the past and had to give way to the industrialists, who triumphed in 1832 politically. In 1846 they got free trade. They knocked out the landlords who were living because of protection. Marx saw the political arena in the country as important. He saw the struggle of economic classes. The lowest class—the working people—were still in an embryonic stage, but to him the Chartist movement was the class of the future.

Landlords, industrialists, and the proletariat. He looked at France and saw the same thing. The nobility in 1830 was unhoused, and its place was taken by the top of the bourgeoisie—he interpreted the July monarchy as the government of the national high bourgeoisie, the bankers and the industrialists. Then in 1848 you had the beginning of the working class revolt. The February

Revolution—the leaders were socialists. There were national workshops. He saw it again in France. In two countries Marx saw the drama of history. Classes stemming from the economic process—to him that uncovered the innermost secret of history. History was a struggle of economic classes. He projected what he saw—in the Middle Ages the same kind of drama, and in the future the same sort of drama will be played. Capitalism itself will develop a working class and will, in following its own purposes, send many peasants into the cities and make them into factory workers. The middle class will lose out and become factory workers.

The February Revolution and so forth were just a flash in the pan and could not hold their own. That was just the beginning, but capitalists see to it that the subordinate actor will eventually become the principal actor. You have, then, this sequence—*the class sequence.* When the proletariat is strong enough it will take over. A dictatorship, although a temporary affair, once assured that the old class of rule is liquidated with no further danger of counter-revolution, finds no further need for the state. The state exists just so one economic class can rule over another. When this is no longer true, the state then withers away.

The Marxist theory of economic class has the role of making history. All of history, then, is a struggle of classes, and these are the economic classes.

This whole conception is a nineteenth-century conception. It is based on developments in England and France and a deduction of the rest of history to the economic class as history-making. In this conception, sixteenth-century England was becoming a great world power. She defeated other powers. England's merchants were pushing off the boards all Continental competitors. There was a duel for decades between the merchant adventurers of England (a national guild of traders) and her rival Hamburg (the merchants of Hamburg). Prior to that time, the German merchants lived in England proper. In the fourteenth and fifteenth centuries German merchants controlled English trade. In the sixteenth century the English merchants gained control. In the sixteenth century there was a rise of the national monarchy, ambitious to establish colonists, and the rise of British merchants.

From a Marxist standpoint, the interpretation of the period was that a new economic class had arisen—the merchant capitalist—who traded abroad. The most important thing to Marxism is the rise of industry, trade, and the merchant capitalist. They shade the policy of government. The expansionist policy of England was shaped by the merchant capitalist, the bourgeoisie.

I would interpret the period as a partnership between the political and the monarchy. In this partnership, the senior partner was the monarchy, with national ambition to help England expand. The junior partner was the merchant adventurers, who worked in well with the monarchy. Some of the most effective agents were merchants who understood trade. In my interpretation, you do not build on just one factor. The merchant was important because he was dynamic and imparted information to the government of England. But he had no control. The Stuart kings came in later and they looked backward. It was the policy of the monarch that decided where things were going.

What was wrong with the German merchants? Nothing. They understood the future, trade, and business. But they had one weakness—no government on which they could rely. They had the Holy Roman Empire, or a part of it, but the government was not interested in trade. Thus the German merchants, the Hanseatic League, lost out. The English merchants had a monarchical partner, and that is why they won out.

We can look at a later situation. Holland in the seventeenth century was the wealthiest nation. She was a great commercial and naval power. She lost to England. She lost out because the necessary political formation was lacking. Also, Holland was involved in the struggles of the Continent, and England was a mere twenty-one miles away.

The economic history interpretation, that of the economic classes, is a product of the nineteenth century. After the nineteenth century, government had stepped aside; you had laissez faire. In the eighteenth century the legislative economic system was permitted to fall into disuse. Merchants and manufacturers did not want to be restricted by apprentice laws and the like. In the eighteenth century government was pushed out of the economic life. During the first half of the nineteenth century government stepped out of the economic picture, and thus the economic actors had the arena to themselves. Marx was looking at the England of 1830 and could say that here are the entities that make history.

But how is it now? In our situation economic life is at a standstill. Chronic depression and unemployment are rife. The business system cannot offer full employment. Now government is brought in and actually is invited back. It came in as a ruling partner. A struggle over who should control government. The middle class saw no prospects in the future. It ran the organization—even the military if necessary—and beat up anyone in the way. Look to the future. That is the situation now.

LECTURE 8
A Critique of Lenin's Theory of the State

The theory of the state was discussed the last two or three times. Today a critique of the Leninist theory of the state will be presented.

What is there about the essence of the Marxist and Leninist system of state that seems to me not realistic? In essence the state is looked upon as a crystallized entity which represents a program in action of a particular ruling class. A state is the executive committee of the ruling class, and that is of primary essence. The executive committee of the capitalist class—outside of Russia. The state is the tool of finance capital in advanced countries. In less advanced countries like China the Marx-Lenin theory would be that the government is bourgeois, but progressive. The role of the Chinese bourgeoisie is to unify the nation and thereby to expand the productive forces of China, and the Chinese government is to be viewed with a favorable eye because it is allied with Russia. The Marxist viewpoint was to support the Chinese government, but since it is a bourgeois government, there is no assurance it will continue indefinitely. Support may be withdrawn when conditions make it possible to replace the bourgeois government with a communist government.

Outside Russia, government was one of finance capital or one dominated by a youthful government bourgeoisie. Support may be withdrawn overnight if one can make a communist government. The attitude toward a bourgeois government is to look after it, as cannibals feed their missionaries well. Perhaps the missionaries realize the fate in store for them and this causes the loss of their Christian attitude. This, then, is the theory—a government that is not socialistic or communistic is a capitalistic government and capitalism constitutes its principal character.

Government is a far more complicated phenomenon that cannot be explained by the above formula. Take, for example, the government of the United States. How can you compress it into the narrow framework of such a formula? You cannot compress it into that particular formula.

The New Deal is not a phenomenon in politics and government that can be described accurately in the Leninist communist sense. To me it is a fluid phenomenon. There was a humanitarian nucleus to increase social security. The President has a gift for making the underprivileged feel that their woes are his woes.[1] He can convince labor and the unemployed that he is really concerned and that it is not just for political effect. That is what makes it possible for him to get a mass answer. This is one constituent of the New Deal—humanitarianism. The President has succeeded in convincing numbers of people that he is a friend of the unemployed as well as all others. It has been a prominent constant in the last eight or nine years. That is what made it possible for Roosevelt to snatch the leadership of labor from Lewis. The President was able to snatch the leadership, but he could not have done so if it had not been for his ringing sincerity in understanding woes.

Another is the organization of groups—organized labor. They derive benefits and advantages from the administration. On the whole, the administration

1. President Franklin Delano Roosevelt.

gets considerable support from the farmers and the foreign-born people, who feel Roosevelt does not look down on them because they belong to a different race. Roosevelt, the aristocrat, makes the foreign feel as good as Americans who have been here for centuries.

In the administration there is also a capacity to overcome dogmatism and squeamishness. The President works with the South. The administration knows the South and knows it is a solid South and so it must work with the South. The administration raises wages throughout the country and also gives the South such things as the Tennessee Valley Authority.

Also the administration shows a lack of squeamishness as far as corrupt machines in the cities are concerned. A lack of squeamishness is highly desirable because it is the only way to get something done. The administration needs mass support. It could never stay in power and put the legislation through that it is getting without political bosses such as Kelly.[2] This is merit really, the capacity to forego squeamishness, deal with people with whom you have to deal. The result is that this administration is able to get progressive legislation, and this is far more than a farmer-labor party in office would have gotten.

After this description, what would you say is the nature of American government? Does it fit a Marxist-Leninist formula? Would you call it capitalistic government? It is a deviation and supports Russia? No, this is not realistic. In realistic depicting you are dealing here with something that does not fit into the formula. It is a political phenomenon not strictly determined by economic class relationships. It is an unhitched horse that wanders over the meadow. And it is a wise animal and knows where it can get the greenest grass and negotiate its business, but it is primarily concerned with reorganizing the meadow to make more furrows.

It is my conviction that there are two kinds of simple-minded people—those who believe everybody and those who believe nobody. I scrutinize. I am not aided by any rigid formula. I am aided to some extent by the insistence of economic group interest in politics as being important, but it is just one aid. I do not think anyone can give you or me an intellectual capsule that will contain the truth. We all are in search for such an intellectual capsule. If we had it there would be no need for research and asking coneself questions. That would be attractive. Then you would not have to doubt or question. That is the tendency of the age. I discussed this with the Webbs, who are great researchers. They agreed with me that research was not popular. Young people want capsules. They do not want to go and find out things for themselves; they want capsules—something in a hurry. The Marxist and Leninist system offers you just that—certainty. If something does not fit, some writer can reconcile the contradiction with theory. To me this formula is not suffi-

2. The Kelly-Nash political machine.

cient. I do not find that it helps very much to the understanding of this present situation. It is more possible to view in the naive terms I have described.

My insistence is that *we cannot look upon politics merely as a reflection of economics.* It has an independent existence. The nuclei under our own conditions may come from a humanitarian group, and it knows how to use vested interests and produce progressive legislation. It may come from a blood-thirsty group. With the aid of psychology of individuals and groups, it may convert a small group and eventually become a totalitarian state.

In each instance, the nucleus group results in powerful political action. It is a political grouping which plays with economic groups. Thus I deviate from Marx. I do not resolve politics into economics only. No doubt economics is important, but politics is not just a reflection of economics—*it is independent action and can take the initiative.*

Now, of course, the trend is planned economy. The question today is, Is the group in the driver's seat to be the inheritors of our civilization, whether they be humanitarians or barbarians? It makes a vast amount of difference whether the integrated economy is presided over by inheritors or by those who deny it.

Politics is far more important than just a reflection of economic class interest.

THE ROLE OF NATIONALISM

The greatest force in the last two or three hundred years has been the force of nationalism, and we do not learn much about it by absolving it in economics—as the rising bourgeoisie rising up and pulling wool over the eyes of people who follow. Nationalism is too big a phenomenon to be compressed into that formula. The rising bourgeoisie plays a part in nationalism but it does not exhaust it. For instance, the two rising nationalisms of Germany and the United States—in such phenomena you had present the factor of a rising middle class; it wanted to play first fiddle. In America there were the rising merchants who smarted under the privileges of the London merchants, but as the phenomenon unfolded itself, it became the American Revolution and the rise of the United States with an impetus toward liberalism throughout the world. This influenced Latin America and Europe.

Contrast this with the consummation of German nationalism as a result of three successfully fought, aggressive wars.[3] The middle-class professionals dream of a united but liberal Germany—it was snatched from their hands by Prussian militarism, by Bismarck. Germany fought Denmark, Austria, and France. In the last war there was lying and distortion by a political genius so that he succeeded, and it was manifested in the crowning of the German em-

3. The Danish War (1864), the Seven Weeks' War (1866), and the Franco-Prussian War (1870-71).

peror in Versailles. The effect was to give fiber to militarism. Russia introduced militarism because it was impressed by the German militarism.

In each instance you are dealing with a national movement resulting in unification. But what a vastly different effect! China is an example of national self-realization on the American pattern rather than on the German pattern. China was fighting aggression, and she now is the spokesman for colonial possessions. The Emperor of China goes to India and tells the British what to do with India. China has moral prestige just as the United States had early in the nineteenth century when she aided the Latin American countries in their nationalism. In each instance you had present the factor of the capitalist class. The Chinese capitalists prior to 1931 (the Chinese merchants) influenced China's nationalism by their class interest. However, when Japan took over the industries, Chinese nationalism was not snuffed out. The Chinese retreated into the interior. The people carried things with them. Chinese nationalism was growing much stronger than ever before, even though the merchant capitalist was subtracted from it. Thus nationalism was not exhausted; it was constituted by the rising bourgeoisie.

Nationalism is a political phenomenon that cannot be compressed into a Marxist formula. I have abandoned Marx, but I am grateful for his shaping me mentally. One should get what one can by way of mental development from that school of thought and go on. But do not turn back on Marxism spitefully.

PART FOUR
Imperialism and War

LECTURE 9
Structural Changes in Capitalism and
Lenin's Idea of Imperialism

So far in the lectures, I have concentrated on two subjects: (1) the materialistic conception of history, and (2) the politics of Marx's theory of state and revolution.

The next subject is the structural changes in capitalism—in capitalistic society. There are two ways of handling subjects—descriptively and analytically. If descriptive, you merely describe phenomena; for instance, point out that in capitalistic society production is concentrated in larger and larger units. So we formulate or describe that change and call it the concentration of capital. In doing so, we are merely acting descriptively. If you point out that the course of development in capitalistic society involves depressions, and crises tend to become more and more severe and prolonged, that is also descriptive. Or if you point out that the control of industry tends to pass from the industrialist (technologically trained) to the financier or banker (banker control of industry), this is just describing.

Handling things analytically is different; this comes later. To handle subject matter analytically—to treat the phenomenon of the concentration of capital or growing depressions analytically—in the Marxist way would be to apply Marx's theory of value, the tendency of the rate of profit to decline, et cetera. Analytically one takes in the economic theory of the Marxist brand.

At present I will merely discuss the descriptive side, pointing out the tendencies in capitalism toward structural changes that Marx pointed out and from which he drew certain conclusions. There is a tendency toward the concentration of capital in larger and larger units and the absorption of the smaller units. This has social and economic consequences. It tends to awaken. As structural capitalism changes from small to big business, it is found to have political repercussions and results in the melting away of the middle class. Marx points

35

out these structural changes descriptively, but still brings us to the conclusions of the consequence of class struggle.

The tendency of capitalistic society is to engender more and more profound economic depressions. It is the consequence of class struggle. Under the impact of depressions you find that victims will react in the direction of being more revolutionary. A mere pointing out of structural changes without giving the analytical leads us to conclusions of great practical significance.

The method is found in Lenin's book on *Imperialism.* It is the one I use today. You find a mere descriptive treatment of the subject. When capitalism reaches its last phase, according to Lenin, it is imperialism.

Where did Lenin get his information? He wrote it shortly after the outbreak of World War I. It was written as a political pamphlet. Where did he get his facts? From two sources, two writers, one of whom was the Englishman J. A. Hobson, an economist of great renown but not an orthodox or revolutionary economist. He was a left-wing progressive and published his book, *Imperialism,* around 1902. The other source of Lenin's book is a German, Rudolf Hilferding, who published his *Finance Capital* in 1910. He was one of the ministers of the Republic and some months ago was detained by the Gestapo. He was killed. He was found hanging. Hilferding gives a description of the structure of capitalism in Germany. The banks had greater control over industry in Germany than in England or the United States.

(a) The factual hinterland of Hobson's book: Hobson was a left-wing liberal and viewed with alarm the attack made by England on the Boer republics, republics in Africa settled by Dutch immigrants and governing themselves according to the Bible. Gold mines and diamond mines were discovered which attracted foreign promoters—English as well as a good many Jews. The foreign promoters found themselves cramped by the style of government in the Bible-reading republics. The foreign promoters were treated as aliens. The result was an attack on the republics and the absorption of the republics into British South Africa. Hobson viewed this with horror. It was unholy and undemocratic. He also observed other wars. The war against China, the 1900 international expedition due to the so-called Boxer Rebellion. Missionaries were killed. England, France, the United States, Russia, and Japan took part in the expedition into China. The two best behaved armies in the war were the Japanese and the Americans. It was an international expedition against China. It was obvious that the killing of foreigners and aliens of any kind was merely a pretext for grabbing spheres of influence. The evident drive behind the venture into China issued from certain groups of businessmen that wanted to make high profits. So you had here, then, a series of such little wars, you might call them, or wars of one particular type, imperialistic wars to enhance the profits of the capitalists.

There was the Spanish American War of 1898 and North America's sway over the small Central American states and island states. Here again, the same phenomenon as the Chinese venture and the South African venture. Capitalists made a good thing of military undertakings, and in many instances instigated military action.

Hobson used this fact. He had to explain why imperial wars were so thick at that time. He said that in advanced industrial countries capitalism had reached a monopolistic stage and monopolistic industries did not care to invest profits in enlarging plants in the mother country as that would spoil their monopolistic position. If you increase plants, then you would have to sell at a lower price and relinquish part of the profits. Thus you seek investment opportunities abroad, especially in those parts of the world rich in natural resources and politically helpless. Thus master regions and capitalists go and exploit natural resources and the population for the purpose of profits. That was Hobson's interpretation of the push toward imperialism.

Hobson's conclusion was to raise wages and increase social services and to do so by taxing the surplus profits of large capitalistic concerns, thereby draining off resources of extra capital. If you did not, capital would drive in the direction of imperialism. So Hobson said to head off imperialism and war by draining off, through taxation, these extra profits. Thereby the standard of the working people would be improved and the political drive of a government into foreign ventures would be headed off. Hobson's ideas led him to a reformist program.

That was the contribution Hobson made to Lenin's theory of imperialism. Lenin took it over.

(b) Hilferding's book gave a picture of industry dominated by banks.

What did Lenin do with the contributions of these two books? He constructed his own theory of imperialism. Lenin pointed out that there are two periods in the development of capitalism. The first period is *competition, individualistic capitalism.* But by and by the tendency of concentration sets in and the result is the second period, *monopoly capitalism.* Then Lenin described several attributes of monopoly capitalism: first, the dominant group is no longer the technician, the industrialist; it becomes banker capitalism, the banker who serves as a midwife in producing monopolies. He consolidates into trusts and other like arrangements, resulting in monopolistic capitalism. When the banker has done that, he does not relinquish his control. The board of directors is the first to prevent the new structure from collapsing. The second is the banker, whose profit is derived from acting as the middleman—and he wants to be sure that he continues as the middleman for the future. The banker hangs on and continues to control the mergers he called into existence.

In the end you find this whole capitalistic system is controlled by a few large banks. That is the picture of finance capital. Monopoly capitalism then is also finance capitalism.

Another attribute Lenin points out is that it is a capitalism which refuses to invest surplus earnings at home for fear of undermining its own monopoly at home. Thus there is an interest in foreign investment opportunities. (An analysis of Lenin here shows he follows Hobson.)

Thus, seeking foreign investments and trying to make foreign investments safe and render profits, the monopoly capitalists at home find it essential to extend political domination over the lands where their investments are. They retain the naked government formerly in power, but it is a "stooge" or rubber stamp, a local ruler or king. But the real power is in the hands, say, of the British adviser. He whispers advice into the ear of the Sultan, and the Sultan knows it is best to follow the advice. One *form of imperialism is to keep the local ruler and control, or have other colonial organizations.*

Thus imperialism comes about, and with it the tendency for several imperial (industrial) countries to divide the whole world among themselves. The industrially backward countries are divided into zones of influence or there is direct division by the industrial countries. The remainder of the world is divided into capitalistic empires.

Such a division of the world among several capitalistic industrial countries is an unstable arrangement. It is not a permanently peaceful arrangement; but will break out in war, one against another.

Capitalistic countries start out as capitalistic at different periods. England was the first industrial capitalistic country and the first imperial country. Germany was a latecomer and could only pick up the leavings. When she came to be a capitalistic country, she was capable of exports, et cetera, as England was, but the choicest morsels were already picked up by England—who got the fattest worms.

An even later-comer was Japan. Industrialism in Japan dates from the First World War. She could never find enough elbow room in the imperial world. For that reason Lenin said that several imperialisms can never remain at peace. They fall out, and that means that war is inevitable. The older imperial countries are unwilling to give up possessions to the latecomers, and war thus is inevitable. To Lenin, war was the clashing of capitalists.

There are other attributes. Lenin points out that there is a tendency toward stagnation, an impounding of productive forces in capitalistic countries. Capitalism is fearful of giving inventive forces free range. When capital is still competitive, then advanced methods of production are used. During the competitive phase capitalism is technically progressive. But when there is monopolistic capitalism and no fear of competition to motivate the installation of better machines, then there is stagnation. Politically controlled industry finds protection by putting inventions on ice. There is a tendency toward stagnation in capitalism.

He observed a tendency for the mother country, or the original capitalistic country, to transfer production to colonies and to develop a leisure class at home—sort of home country resorts, et cetera. There was a tendency toward possession, toward the good things of life. Lenin said this is characteristic of the more advanced industrial countries.

Still another tendency is to corrupt the uppermost layers of the labor class. The members are bribed into acquiescence by having wages and standards of living raised. The standards of the bulk of the working class go down. The upper layer is detached from the rest of the working class as a result of deliberate bribery in the form of a higher standard of living and making them satisfied. It is a wholesale corruption of the upper layer of the working class.

Lenin's recipe is revolution. Transform imperial wars into proletarian revolutions. That was his policy during the First World War—to overthrow all belligerent governments and have a world-wide revolution. If corrupt leaders stand in the way, kick them out and have revolutionary leadership; he had the proletariat as the victor.

This is the sum and substance of the gist of Lenin's theory of imperialism. The emphasis is on the connection between capitalistic rivalries and wars. Wars today stem from capitalistic rivalries. That is the gist of Lenin's theory—under capitalism war is inevitable. There is no possibility to stave off war by a peaceful division of the world. The countries are bound to fall out. Today war stems from imperialism. The war going on now is treated as between two rival imperialisms.

LECTURE 10
Kautzky's Ideas and a Presentation of
Plebeian Imperialism

IMPERIALISM

Last time I gave a summary of Lenin's idea of imperialism. In Lenin's book there is a rather caustic statement about Kautzky. Kautzky was the outstanding Social Democrat in 1890. The party broke, and he then ceased to be the theoretician of the whole movement and became the theoretician of the right-wing or center. The left-wing went to Lenin. The center of gravity of the theory is that under capitalism war is inevitable. Capitalism, composed of monopolies, bankers, and capitalists, then, is under compulsion to seek foreign investment opportunities, and investment takes place in colonial countries, and that in turn leads to the extension of political domination or empire-building. The center of gravity of the theory is that there cannot be such a thing as peaceful imperialism. Divide the world into spheres of influence, but that peaceful solution cannot stay put. This is because countries are not in the same position. Some have developed early and others are latecomers. The choice morsels have gone to the older countries. Even an old country's tempo of development is not even; it is subject to abrupt change. Sooner or later there is a violent falling-out among the imperialistic countries, and that means war. Lenin said it is up to the revolutionary proletariat to use the imperialistic wars to put over the proletariat revolution; in doing so, of course, obstacles would be encountered. Some of the proletariat would turn traitor to the revolutionary proletariat class. They would be beneficiaries of imperialistic capitalism; they would get positions, favors, et cetera. Not only leaders, but more skilled workers, the aristocracy of labor, would benefit. The capitalists would see to it that this upper strata is separated from the rest of the proletariat. Consequently, it is one's duty to liquidate these influences and expel the opportunists and see to it that a pure proletariat spirit has full sway over the group. That is the Leninist theory.

Kautzky tries to bypass war and revolution and get international socialism by peaceful means, by avoiding war and internal revolution. First, he poses the possibility of a unified world-wide structure under a capitalistic system. By international organization they may work out a framework of an international order. To Kautzky, imperialism does not necessarily lead to war. He does not say that war will not occur—it can because of foolishness, but there does not have to be war. Bring society to a higher level, permit productive forces greater sway—that is how to bypass war.

Bypass revolution by painting a picture of peaceful democratic revolution in each capitalistic country. The process is as follows. A strong labor movement, organized politically, with unions, et cetera, becomes the guide of the lower middle-class groups. The labor movement is a nucleus of a wider democratic movement. It embraces the lower groups and thereby labor succeeds by stepping into government by way of a coalition with the lower middle-class groups. The coalition embraces other democratic parties. The coalition government steps into office and begins to democratize institutions such as transport, coal mining, et cetera. At the same time, look after the interests of the farmers and small shopkeepers. Democratic coalition under the leadership of the labor proletariat can bypass revolution. That is what Kautzky says—bypass war and revolution.

During the twenties, there began to be a wide publication of Lenin's ideas. Beginning in 1916 or 1917, Lenin's ideas show a real intellectual struggle with Kautzky's. The schools of thought of the time were Lenin's, Kautzky's, and the Social Democrats'. Discussion turned on the particular issue as to whether imperialism can construct a world-wide framework without breaking up into war. The other issue was, Can you have socialization of society without a proletariat revolution?

In all of the discussions there was one common basis. While there were opposite views, they were building with the same entities. For instance, *finance capital.* They differed as to the behavior of finance capital or labor or the proletariat. While they arrived at opposite conclusions, they used the same concepts and entities and both remained true to the materialistic concept of history—history is a class struggle, et cetera. The basic concept is pretty much the same. The principal actors were the proletariat and the capitalist.

Thus imperialism was conceived of as being capitalistic imperialism. Lenin said it is imperialism that will break up in war. Kautzky said that imperialism need not be so bellicose—it can be constructive. Both talked of capitalistic imperialism and said that the dynamics in society was capitalistic imperialism.

PLEBEIAN IMPERIALISM

This concept is alien to both Kautzky and Lenin. It is an imperialism of a group not prompted by profits; it has for its drive that the whole people are to become the ruling race, the master race. That is not an accurate description of a particular country, but use your imagination. Suppose such an imperialism were possible, what would it look like and actually be? A nation which looks upon itself as a master race! Other races would be inferior and must be kept in place for the master race. Assume that everyone belonging to the master race would be appealed to—promoted to a higher station in life, not only a better paying job, but a higher psychological station too. The master race feels superior. Supposing, then, such a master race wanted to guard against any comeback or revolution from an inferior race, it would try to deindustrialize countries inhabited by inferior races, because for a country to have industry, there must be ideas. Take machinery and put it in communities where there is the master race. The inferior races are given common labor jobs, unskilled work. Have them prepare the food and raw materials for the master race. The next step in order to perpetuate the masters is to see to it that the inferiors do not have an intelligentsia. The maximum education available to the subject races would be just the common education needed to read and write and figure in their own language. Do this so that they do not develop leadership. Leaders of the master race, since they are students of history, know that in the past master races lost out because they became soft and luxury-loving. They see to it that their own people are not soft; they are brought up like Spartans with hard and physical regimens. The government of the master race is reared upon the leadership principle. See to it that you pick out young people of the master race to be trained and brought up to be leaders. There is also a pretty careful picking over and elimination of the unfit. The training of the ruling group is self-centered so that it would never permit inferior races to raise their heads. Among the master race, differences in income would be held down so as to prohibit corruption. This is a picture—a speculation.

More realistically, let us assume Nazi Germany. Of course it is corrupt and not Spartan, but in many regards it has carried out such a plan. The Nazis have taken industries from subject races and eliminated a goodly share of educated people among the subject races. They also have done a good deal of training for leadership of the master race itself. In recruiting those destined for positions they did not follow old class lines. The old ruling classes were not eliminated but were permeated by the newer elite. Important positions were given more and more to those from the dominant party, and in picking for leadership, the choice was from the lower classes. This was because they had no foreign blood in their veins. They have racial purity and from here the new leaders must be recruited.

The picture given above is the ideal, the fanciful, with no corruption. We know many in the Nazi party knew how to make money and acquire wealth. But let us imagine that the Nazi German finds himself fighting for his life with his back to the wall. Today it is still very doubtful that this is the case. But let us assume that the campaign of the summer and spring fails and the Russian menace is greater and the Western allies start doing things so that the existing German finds himself up against it. Then there will be a lot of corruption cleaned up. Those who got wealthy would be made to put their wealth into the treasury of the nation. Every German fighting in the army would know that defeat would be something terrible for himself and for his country. Victory would be grand and one might be an administrator in other countries. There would be careers for young people. Careers of adventure and power. On the other hand, defeat means revenge by the subject people, depression, no future. Victory means a grand and glorious career and adventure. One could go to other countries, have positions, or one could stay at home and lord it over all. That is what I mean by plebeian imperialism. The nucleus need not be finance capitalists, but young adventurers—in this case, German—just as the idea possibly is in the minds of the Germans in Russia. They are fighting like wildcats in Russia. What deeps them fighting to the bitter end? Is it fear? Hardly. Yet it may be a factor. But more important is that they are fighting for themselves, for their chance to lord it over others. *Very likely the phenomenon we are now confronting* is perhaps closer to the picture I drew rather than to the picture either Lenin or Kautzky drew.

If we are not bound by tradition, by accepted stereotypes, such a picture is not far from the truth. It is a hypothesis that needs to be checked and considered. Furthermore, the conventional view of fascism (that nazism and fascism is finance capital fighting with its back to the wall) played us a dirty trick. Those who point to that view thought that by depicting it as fascism people would oppose fascism and capitalism—as Kautzky claimed. Thus, if told that fascists are fighting for the capitalists, people view them as friends rather than as enemies—simply because they were people friendly to capitalism.

The identification of nazism with capitalism made friends for fascism among the conservative people, the middle class, et cetera. The communists are boring away. The fascists are rough, but after all their hearts are in the right place. Under the menace of communism we accept them because they claim to be for free enterprise.

The second bad effect of that intellectual trend was to deceive us as to the real strength of what we are fighting today. We were given the idea that we do not need to stir ourselves much because Germany will fall from within. So long as we identify nazism with finance capital and imperialism, that gives us an alibi for not bestirring ourselves—we are confident that Germany will collapse from within.

But if you accept my view, then we see that there is a whole people in a crusade for themselves—the plebeian idea. If the German people lose some battles, the German leadership will have to crack down on the wealthy Nazis as greater danger comes. There will be a greater chance that the ideal position of the plebeian will become more of a reality and thus the German fighting spirit would be enhanced.

We are misled by the idea of what constitutes imperialism. I was laughed at for the theory of plebeian imperialism. Now people see what it means. Now when we are up against it, it is our duty not to be content with the conventional theories but we must examine all theories advanced.

LECTURE 11
Job Imperialism

There is an article in the local paper which describes how the German army was taken over by the new power group, the Nazis.[1] This valuable article describes the process of assimilation and taking over. The army officer caste was the ruling group in Prussia for several centuries, and it was that group that was looked up to. A new group, by skill, was able to take over the army caste. The article states that when Hitler was in power, the army officer caste thought it could save its own power by stipulating that there would be no party politics. The young recruit of the army had been a conditioned Nazi. Hitler presented generals with badges in public; thus they really had to accept. Gradually Nazism seeped into the army. The army is now under the control of the Secret Police. The technique for assuming control of the military caste is shown by reading the article.

1. *Capital Times* (Madison, Wisconsin), December 22, 1944, p. 1.

The conventional radical theory of fascism is still that the capitalist group pulls wires. If the group of people who possessed the most valuable training in war—such as the army—if such a group with such a powerful monopoly of ability—if they could be taken over, then how about the capitalist groups? Then, how can we think bankers and capitalists resist being taken over? The special ability that the capitalists possess is ability that is not very valuable. They can read the future; they can make forecasts as to what kind of commodities there will be in the future. That is the most telling function of people like Morgan and others—they can foretell the future. In order to make the proper move in the setup you had to have what no economist or statesman could have. The entrepreneurs were the ones who had it. When the economic future is uncertain, they exercise a sixth sense.

That is why the nineteenth century was the golden age of the Jews. Jews were in business and commerce for centuries and were able to foretell the future. When you have an economy that works for the government or war, this capacity to guess the future correctly is no longer necessary to possess. Where you have an organized war economy, such as Germany has had since 1934, and things are worked out, there is no longer a need to tell the future. The real ability of businessmen, their capacity, does not enter into the picture at all because you work for the government. You make tanks and you know they are needed. The special ability of the capitalist group does not enter at all. The capitalists are "has-beens," so why should we assume this new government based on the monopoly of power which could digest the army could not digest the capitalists?

The most important decision in Germany during the last four or five years was war. The capitalists did not want war, but the decision was made by this new group. A plebeian imperialism—a group of people who play to the idea of the master race. There is corruption but it can be straightened out. When a special appeal has to be made to every German in the army to make the utmost sacrifice, then corruption will stop.

Even during the period of strong capitalism there were many elements in imperialism. *Job imperialism.* In England in the eighties and nineties when Gladstone was in his prime, Gladstonian liberalism scoffed at the empire. The liberals were concerned with free trade, world trade. Imperialism then was under a cloud and it was considered outmoded. Still, the empire kept going. What kept it going? Another element of a tangible nature that kept the empire together: *job imperialism.* Many families whose sons went to the empire for highly paid positions saw the empire as jobs. That was a material interest which helped to keep the empire up. It was not the capitalists, but the bureaucratic interests—the families of the aristocracy. You can see why I am trying to depict job imperialism; it was a chance to have well-paid jobs and to enjoy prestige.

If the Nazi phenomenon succeeds, you will also have job imperialism. A speech by Goebbels told German youth that this is a period in which to live and great jobs are to be had. He appealed to the ambitions, and not necessarily to the upper class but to the lower class as well. The lower class feels it is superior to the upper class because of its pure blood line. You can carry over the job imperialism of England to the German lower and middle class.

Now go back to the hypothesis. More and more, this phenomenon of imperialism is not capitalistic imperialism. It is imperialism, of course, but it is a different story.

The Japanese phenomenon is not a capitalistic imperial phenomenon. Japan started conquering the world market. She paid low wages and possessed industrious people. Japan has a class accustomed to hard, steady labor. The Japanese industrialists had it nice. They had a laboring class that did not have to be sweetened. They were ready to use factory discipline. In fact, they were ready for quite new industry—putting in new machinery. Japan was going places after the First World War. Japanese finance capital was coming in and giving other countries a run for their money. I do not know how the Japanese industrialist felt about extending markets. I feel if the military had left the industrialists alone they would not have rushed into war. It was done by the army class. The military has a socialist feeling.

The Japanese army mind seems to run along lines of military socialism. It is military socialism rather than capitalism that they are trying to spread. I am dubious as to whether the industrialists were happy on December 7 when Pearl Harbor occurred. It was a risk—if won, okay, if lost, lose all. The capitalist mind does not work to risk investment or to risk chance. It does not take the risk of sticking a pin into the lion.

I am willing to bet that the people in Japan who decided on the policy were not capitalists, but militarists. They look down on the capitalists, but with a sort of sympathy, a condescending sympathy for the peasant and the soldier (the peasant is a soldier). It is a psychology which is anticapitalist. It is a power group and it imposes its will on all other classes, such as the intellectuals and capitalists. From what I know, the imperialism of the Japanese is not along the lines of the Lenin and Hobson idea.

The Hobson book in 1902 and Lenin's in 1916 reflect the situation just around the turn of the century, and the little wars at that time were capitalistic wars, such as the Boer War, the expedition in China, et cetera. Those wars around the turn of the century were the kind to suggest the Hobson idea. In the First World War it is not so clear. But we know those immediately responsible for its outbreak were not the industrialists and the financiers. The groups that pushed were the emperor of Austria-Hungary and those who pushed the czar of Russia. They were bureaucrats who had an argument to prove, and they wanted to make careers. The Magyars of Hungary and the czarist group in Russia could not be classed as capitalists. The war did come about as the result of imperial rivalries, but take the above into account.

After the war—try to arrive at an understanding—two groups organized were groups of labor and groups of businessmen. Trouble came from the middle class. In Poland the troublemakers were not labor or business but the teachers, the intellectuals, journalists, et cetera. The wave of nationalism in Europe after the armistice was the product of the semi-intellectual (the teacher, the clerk, et cetera)—he wanted to rise and pushed the national claims.

The first sensible agreement between Germany and France was between two capitalists—two capitalists who tried to inject common sense. We know that labor did not strive for war. Labor and business really were not so much to blame for what happened. They could not overcome the intellectuals.

That is the way I interpret the immediate past and the immediate present, and it strengthens my hypothesis. I think capitalist imperialism is based on what is true at the turn of the century.

PART FIVE
A Critique of Marx

LECTURE 12
Perlman's Interpretation of History

Today I am going to discuss my interpretation of history. I have left Marxism. But I do not feel superior to it or bitter against it, but grateful. I will discuss an interpretation of history paralleling Marx's interpretation, and it is built largely on Marx.

My interpretation of history is that the concrete person stands in the center of the arena, as it were. I do not like abstractions, such as the proletariat and the bourgeoisie, the concept that history is an abstract mass and abstract force and it is in the political arena. Instead, one should study the concrete conduct of laborers, farmers, employers, and others. This is the better approach because it gives you a chance for greater accuracy. The class or group Marxism considers the solid group, in practical operation is not so solid but it divides up. Divisions in the proletariat are not just backsliding. In organized labor one sees why they have played a conservative role in the last twenty-five years rather than a revolutionary role.

I am grateful to Marx for concepts, but I think it is much safer not to be content with *abstract* concepts. Marxist concepts of the proletariat and the bourgeoisie when first formulated as representing history-making entities were a step in advance for those times because people had felt that history meant the action of great men only—they were men who were free. The Marxist formulation of what were history-making entities was a step in advance. If we conceive of history as solely the product of great men, then there is no basis for predicting conduct. Marx's stress on economic classes was a step forward; it was a realistic approach when compared to the mysticism other schools of thought preached. Marxism with an emphasis on economic classes was a powerful injection of realism into historical thinking. But in presuming to isolate history-making entities, we must go a step further. Study groups in actual life and conduct and thereby get closer to what motivates them.

Marx's concept of the proletariat is a historical force, a great historical role—

47

the role of destroying institutions of the capitalistic order and the setting up of proletariat institutions. In the Marxist conception, the proletariat is a historical force with a definite role to play. Its part is determined by the historical part. If, at any moment or turn, the actor in the play substitutes a line, then from the Marxist view the conclusion is that the actor had been bribed by a hostile force and failed in fulfilling his historical role.

That is the role of the historical groups in the Marxist conception. They have a role laid down before them and the lines they speak are given to them by the historical process. The actor's own feelings as a concrete human are not allowed to enter. Scholarship, from a Marxist view, says that it is futile to determine the actor's thoughts. The actor is predetermined. The impression is that addressing one's self to the phenomenon of the wage-earner to find out what is in his mind and what he is after, is foolish according to Marx. That is why I broke with Marx. I do not feel that the play was written a long time ago and that it is futile to find out what the worker is thinking. I try to study the worker's mind. I try to deduce what is in his mind, what he wants to do, and what does or does not stir him. Make an empirical investigation of groups. You do not assume that of necessity economic groups have in mind the cause and that it is written in their minds; but investigate and study history of organizations, how they work, what their code of conduct is, et cetera. From the study of working rules, the code of conduct and values, you find out what is in workers' minds and formulate a theory of the labor movement. They are not stooges of history but write their own lines. They act in a manner of their own. They develop their own values, lines, and code of conduct.

You find that what they are concerned with primarily is not to make history but to obtain certain improvements, to enrich their lives in the material and spiritual sides. On the economic side, they wish to overcome economic insecurity; on the spiritual side, they wish to overcome subjection to other humans, such as foremen and employers.

They are Tom, Dick, and Harry—without an idea of what their role should be, but they are out to seek something they want. They do not want to be pushed around. They do not want to be slaves or underlings, but to have rights of their own.

That is where my approach differs from Marxism. Marx, when he formulated his theory, was aiming at the same thing. In Marx's mind, concrete objectives of labor coincided with the making of history. To him concrete objectives, such as the trade unions, were training schools for the role the proletariat was to play. Marx was not contemptuous of concrete objectives; that is why he encouraged trade unions. But he felt concrete objectives would of necessity be glorified and lead up to the grand objective of the performance of the historical role.

Marx was a student of the labor movement, but the labor movement organizations of his day—trade unions and cooperatives—were intellectual and humble. The concrete organizations were without protest to the intellectual leaders from the upper classes like Marx. The certainty of concrete objectives was bound to find ultimate expression in the proletariat revolution. That was brought out by the humility of the organizations in the first phase of development. They were spiritually dependent upon revolutionary intellectuals like Marx. Later, when the organizations grew and developed, they gradually but surely tended to emancipate themselves from the tutelage of the intellectual. In Germany that took place in 1905 and 1906. In 1905, the year of the Russian Revolution, I saw the first revolution at the age of seventeen. It was the biggest thing on the social horizon and it had tremendous repercussions in Germany. Slogans and ideas of the German Social Democrat party were the ideas of the *Manifesto*. Here the Russian Revolution, with railroad workers, et cetera on general strike in 1905, was so potent that the Russian government yielded. This made an impression on the German Social Democrat party. They began to agitate for the mass strike to be added to the arsenal of weapons for the German Social Democracy. The leadership of the party up to that time did not encourage revolution because it was afraid it would be a chance for the government to break it down.

The Russian Revolution gave hope to the Germans. Luxemburg[1] and other leaders raised the issue of the mass strike as a weapon the German Social Democrats should use. Under the influence of the intellectuals the party did adopt the weapon as one that could be used. This caused an uproar from a quarter where it was not expected. It came from the trade unions. The trade unions in Germany at that time were busy going up. From 1890 on they were doing spade work and were content to let the intellectuals in the Social Democrat party lay down the political policy. Now they were alarmed and criticized the party on grounds of recklessness. Now, due to the Russian Revolution, you say use the strike and play into the hands of the monarchical government. The government will swoop down on us and break us up. The trade unions rose in rebellion against the revolutionary intellectuals who were thinking in line with Marxist terms. Luxemburg was fearless and Marxist. She was surprised at the trade unions. The trade unions developed lines of their own, and again Luxemburg was surprised. The trade unions continued to clamor and criticize the party. It almost came to a rupture, and before the First World War, labor in Germany was not accustomed to such ruptures. So the old leader, Bebel,[2]

1. Rosa Luxemburg (1870-1919), German revolutionary, important in the history of international socialism, and a leader of the Social Democratic party. She attempted to draw profitable conclusions for the German workers from the Russian people's experiences through her leadership and publishing activities.

2. August Bebel (1840-1913), cofounder of the German Social Democratic party and its most influential and popular leader for more than 40 years. Bebel was unwilling to yield to Left wing pressure to indulge in extraparliamentary experiments.

interfered and as a result of the mediator, they formulated an agreement of equal rights, which meant the Social Democrat party no longer would lay down policy and assume that the unions would follow. If the party laid down a new policy, the trade unions could veto it. The trade unions had the veto power over the party. It was a turning point. Here the concrete person was the workingman concerned with the day-to-day recognition, and he could veto.

That made a great impression upon me. It was brought home to me two or three years later. I worked for a socialist writer in the United States. I read German and I had to read debates, and this was a turning point in my thinking about the labor movement—that is, the victory of the concrete point of view over the abstract view. The concrete Tom, Dick, and Harry are the body of the abstract proletariat. That is one of the great divergences between the theory developed here and Marx's theory. In American labor history, the dominance of the concrete point of view is not really challenged.

There are other respects in which I could not follow the material concept of history (I have already said so indirectly in the early lectures): the assumption that only economic classes are history-making entities, the struggle of economic classes, the economic class role as a history-making entity, which rules out other groups are among them. If a political group is in the arena, as a good Marxist you look for an economic group in the woodpile who is pulling strings. Economic classes are essentially solid and do not break up. I came to see that that is an oversimplified picture of the whole thing. You have political groups that make history just as well. A century of expansion due to the economic factor, et cetera—this is the main actor and the government is secondary. With expansion changing and contracting you might have a different situation—political entities coming in. Our own history is a process more resembling the Middle Ages with the monarch and the church being important. I found national entities great history-makers. They have been history-makers ever since the rise of the Renaissance. Here, again, I saw something with my own eyes that drove nationalism into consciousness. I came from a textile town; there were two groups—the Poles and the Jews. The Jews were weavers, handicraftsmen before the Industrial Revolution. During the struggle in Russia the proletariat acted as a unit. But I saw street fights between Jews and Poles. They were fighting for jobs. The Poles said God made factory jobs for the Poles and for the Jews, handicraft. Handicraft was declining due to the factories. It was nationalism working. The Czarist police came in and mediated between the two factions of the proletariat. This was a shock because the proletariat was divided and fighting over jobs. It shocks you out of intellectual complacency.

Such things shock you out of your dogmatism. Of course, one might have taken an easier way and said that the proletariat was incited by government spies, et cetera, and then broke out in an unproletarian way. It is an easy way to believe, but it did not work.

It was not just anti-Semitism or anything of its sort. It touched the mind of the worker and his job consciousness, about which he is most conscious. Where the majority is confronted by the weaker minority, job consciousness impels the majority to come forth with no greater value, namely, than the fact that the better jobs belong to the majority group.

This made me think, and in the sense of modifying my original Marxist concept of history! It made me look for groupings within economic groups. From that, extend toward other economic classes. I found groups devoted to other values, just as to the economic—such as religious, temperance, et cetera. They are all groups and they exert an influence.

LECTURE 13
A Contrast between the Abstract and Concrete Approaches to History

Last time I gave my point of view on an interpretation of history. Now I will contrast the abstract and the concrete approach. We all are concerned with how labor acts. We all are concerned with the theory of labor action and middle-class action. The contribution that Marx made was great and valuable. Marxism directed our attention from abstraction in the clouds to action of the human group. History is not willed by the Supreme but became the handiwork of the human group in pursuit of certain purposes. Marx directed attention to human conduct. The followers of Marx were hypnotized by his categories, i.e., the proletariat and the bourgeoisie. It is granted that Marx's categories were based upon the reading of history or observations he himself made in his own time. These categories were a great advance over what had preceded him.

I look further and try to construct additional categories, especially groups within the categories he enumerated and by further examination of concrete action, for example, by labor. We can observe that since Marx we have discovered that labor does not act as a revolutionary proletariat under all circumstances. Only one proletariat has acted as Marx said and that was the Russian proletariat in the revolution of 1917–21. They were the only ones who acted as a revolutionary proletariat. The German and British trade unionists and the Americans did not act as a revolutionary proletariat should. Thus the problem— why didn't they? That leads one to study the situation and to the framing of the following hypothesis. *It is possible, perhaps, that it is only during the first phase of capitalism—the first phase of capitalistic society—that it has a revolutionary psychology.* In the more advanced countries or where capitalism is more advanced, there is protective labor legislation; and in such countries that are more mature capitalistically, there is a more mature proletariat. The mature proletariat flunks out and becomes the opportunistic proletariat. Marx erred when he gave us the revolutionary proletariat, because this psychology is found only in the immature proletariat. It is under an exploitative propensity of capitalism which is not checked. Once it is checked, the proletariat then is more conservative. In such countries Marx's dictum—the proletariat has nothing to lose but his chains—is not so, because he has *more* to lose. Maybe the gold chains are in the shape of cottages, radios, and the like and some property right which protection unionism throws around the worker's job.

If you continue to look, you will see that you are seeing something the Marxists do not see. You can point out that there is a lot more to the theory of revolutionary action than that the proletariat gets more and more revolutionary as capitalistic society develops, even during the long depression which we had after 1930. Under the Marxist idea you should have expected a proletariat explosion. The depression, however, had a numbing effect on radical action. In England the depression showed the conservative nature of the labor movement. In 1924, 1925, and 1926 labor showed a revolutionary sparkle, but after that there was a swing to the right.

The economic effects of the depression became localized and mitigated. They were localized in the unemployed class on the dole. A few years ago I saw that class in South Wales. It was a permanently unemployed class, especially among the young people. There was no real revolutionary action from them. They were discontented, it is true, but they were kept docile by the dole. Those who were on the dole felt protected—the dole to the unemployed kept up their wages. The observation at close range of the British working class during the depression, and especially workers at the start of life, brought me to observe that the working class does not act as Marx said. It is held in check by the dole and labor legislation, and the others, members of unions, are not forced to take what the employers say because the unemployed are on the dole and they do not affect the wage.

The conclusion is to continue Marx's work in our own day, continue his command of social realization, study groups at close range. I believe it is important that we do this.

The other thing brought home in the last eight or ten years has been the revolutionary stage of the middle class. In Marxist thinking the middle class is not supposed to speak in a loud voice of its own. It does speak in a loud voice. (Marxists were not dumbfounded by this. They have proof against such shocks.) We have to continue Marx's method of realism and keep our eyes peeled for action groups, history-making groups.

I have stressed groups of a noneconomic nature, such as power groups organized politically or militarily or semimilitarily, which come in and dominate.

Such independent power groups in Marxist thinking do not fit—according to Marx, power is economic. But as we go back in history, we find military groups knew how to subject advanced groups. We are out to find more and more history-making groups.

Marxist thinking tends to divide human history into airtight epochs, such as the feudal epoch and so on. The idea underlying this thinking is that our standard of ethics and morality is shaped by each epoch in its own way in accord with the ruling class. Feudal times, feudal morality; in capitalism, capitalistic morality; and so forth. *The effect is to virtually deny that our moral civilization is an accumulative phenomenon.* Then you can assume there is no such thing as an absolute in morality and ethics. Conduct is what is to the advantage of the ruling class. It stamps approval and by propaganda impresses ethics on the populace in general. When the proletariat class is conscious, it throws off the bourgeois morality and comes out with its own proletariat morality—what is right and what is wrong. On the way to power the proletariat is the carrier of morality. This kind of thinking occurs because Marx associates morality with class; that is, whatever is of interest to a class is moral. As with the bourgeoisie, the proletariat considers itself moral in its struggle for power. You get a relativistic morality. It is relative to the interests of a particular class. Under such a system of morality you can take human life. There were mass purges in Russia—they did not stop when Hitler came to power—you had the taking of human life. Once you have relativistic morality there is no such thing as accumulative morality, but morality shaped by the economic class in power or in its struggle for power. This is a sanction to take human life. Marx was opposed to individual terror such as taking the life of anyone, but he opposed it because it was ineffective on the ground that history is made by the masses. If you bump off an individual, if there is mass strength the bumping off of an individual is of no value because some other person takes his place. Marx was opposed to individual terrorism but not to mass terrorism. In the early thirties in Russia, the government uprooted peasants and sent them up to Siberia where many died. This was justified on the ground that the peasants stood in the way of the triumph of the proletariat revolution. It was moral to expedite it. This relativism in ethics leads to human headaches and it paves the way, or sets an example, for a similar departure from our standards on the part of rivals such as the fascists. Often the case is that pupils outdo the teacher. The teacher's responsibility does not disappear because others follow the example and outdo it.

Ethical rule or democracy? We know what the Fascists think of that. Who set the example? Not Mussolini. The first one was set by Lenin in January 1918, when the Constitutional Convention was just elected. Because it did not yield a majority to Lenin's party, the Constitutional Convention was forcibly dissolved. The popular will was set at naught. Moral shock was experienced by the

Russians. The Constitutional Convention was something the liberal Russians
had looked forward to. The hope of the thinking Russians was that the Czar
would fall and the political destinies of the people would be shaped by an
assembly of the people. It was a Constitutional Convention; it was dispersed
by the command of Lenin. That was a precedent. Lenin did that, not because
he was a power-seeker, but because he was convinced historically that the time
had come for a worldwide proletariat revolution. The Russian Revolution was
just a stepping-stone to worldwide revolution. It was felt to be the ethical duty
of the Bolsheviks to disperse the convention because it was an anti-Bolshevik
majority and thus would not provide the match to fire revolutions. Thus there
are two moralities. Lenin was not immoral nor an adventurer. He was highly
moral, but he had the Marxist theory of ethics—anything helpful to the proletariat cause was good ethics. He felt that to prevent Russia and the Constitutional Convention from establishing a peasant democracy was imperative
ethics. We feel it was an unethical step (those of us not following Marx's
ethics). At that time, 85 percent of the Russians were peasants. The proletariat
was small, but Lenin was convinced that the world in general was in a phase of
worldwide proletariat revolution, and that was more important than permitting
the Russians to express the kind of government they must have. Lenin operated
from an abstraction—the proletariat revolution. In the concrete, the proletariat
countries at the time insisted on expressing themselves differently. In 1918 in
Britain the proletariat was fighting the First World War for the British, and so,
too, in other countries. Lenin operated from an abstraction of the proletariat.
He knew there had to be a celestial body, because it was written by the historical process to take ethics from the celestial body which possessed the mass, and
that other bodies would bow to it. That was an abstraction. If it had been
pointed out to Lenin that he was abstract, he would have argued.

To him, the thing to smash was budding democracy in Russia. To me, it was
the will and intention of concrete humans. The way to ascertain what the
masses wish is to take a vote or let them express themselves clearly, or by the
action they are taking.

The abstract and the concrete are what I am illustrating. If you take the concrete ethical theory, that is, something worked out by groups of concrete
humans that have to work out problems of the day, you find that the ethical
is not just something relative to a particular epoch in history, but something
that throughout history we have grown and accumulated from one period to
the next. The precious thing is the regard of the human individual. He is a
concrete entity. He is a product of the whole civilizing process. Ethics are not
discontinued from one epoch to another, but if we look on this as an accumulative process, then we must deny relativism. (We are not so shocked when we
see it as Lenin did—to go ahead with the proletariat view and not personal
power. But we are shocked when we see those who go ahead on their own.)

LECTURE 14
*A Discussion of Lewis Corey's
"The Unfinished Task"*

I have read the galley proof of Lewis Corey's new book.[1] He has written several books. At first he was a true Marxist, now he has deviated. His thinking runs pretty much on the things I have told you. It is the present situation and the way out. The book stresses the process of power formation. It is a book that shows a political consciousness. It is conscious of the value of democracy. The greatest calamity he envisions is the union of economic and political power in the hands of the same group of people. He finds them in Russia and among the Fascists. He found them in an earlier period in the absolutism of the early seventeenth century. He says that where economic and political power are united it means slavery.

How do you describe the real content of Fascism in terms of power? Fascism is the union of political and economic power. It began by playing with monopoly capitalism, but when it became self-confident it discarded the original capitalists. Fascism to Corey is a bureaucratic military formation. I call it a political-military formation. Fascists make use of bureaucrats but are not bureaucratic themselves. I call Fascists political adventurers. Corey agrees with my analysis of Fascism, but he does not identify it with old capitalism. He says that it starts with old monopoly capitalism. Fascism uses the capitalists and enslaves them. For a time they are in a gilded cage and make profits, but they cannot re-invest. The Fascists used the capitalists as the church used the Jews in the Middle Ages. The church prohibited usury at first (the Jews were usurers), but did not allow the Jews to dispose of their earnings—the medieval kings used them. The Fascists use the finance capitalists in much the same way.

Another idea Corey had I thought was good, that historically, political freedom sprang from the diffusion of property. People prospered and accumulated property (manufacturing). It was the basis for demanding political rights. Under the feudal system property and government were one, and there was no such thing as political rights for the masses. There was the rise of a class of small property owners, holders, that used property for self-support in enterprises. That was the basis for political freedom. Property gave them an independent base. Their livelihood was not controlled.

In the society of the future, Corey does not want to see a blanket of nationalization of property and industry. He lays store on the survival of small property owners, such as the farmer. The farm has retained its usefulness, and that must be protected. Corey is for individual enterprise and ownership in agricul-

1. *The Unfinished Task: Economic Reconstruction for Democracy* (New York: Viking Press, 1942).

ture. This contrasts with Russia, where farming is collectivized. He is afraid of a government that is too strong—he means a government that controls the livelihood of too many people. He would do away with monopoly capitalism but would not replace it by government control. He would arrange for *public operations.* That is, he would have the monopolized industries taken over and made into public corporations. He does not want the government to appoint management. He wants functional management to be given a preponderance of authority in the public corporations. He does not describe how to give the people the original mandate, but he is certain that the government should not make appointments. A minority of directing should be in the hands of organized labor and other groups like cooperatives and their like.

The other thing is the emphasis on the deliberate intention to divide power among organized groups and organized labor. The government proper should be a partisan of Congress. Corey says that concentration of power in the hands of the executive is dangerous. He does not approve of government by the expert—it leads to Fascism. He thinks you need a congressional check.

He thinks we are in our present difficulty because of structural changes in capitalism from a small scale to a monopoly that exploits. Monopoly profits at present cannot be re-invested as in the past. In the past, re-investment took place because of expansion, and that took capital. From time to time there is a breakdown; but with such periodic breakdowns the organism, economic society, gets out of the crisis by investment. In the stage of monopoly capitalistic profits you accumulate on a large scale, but with technology we do not need much capital. Our present trouble is brought about by monopoly capitalism with huge profits. Prices are monopolistic, and you have huge profits. In competitive capitalism profits found a place for investment again. With monopoly there is no demand for investment. Thus, chronic depression is permanent. The permanent economic crisis has precipitated social crises and Fascism.

In his social analysis of Fascism and his formulation of power in society, he fears the union of economic and political power in the same group. He says that we must remedy the situation by dispersing the power first to the small-scale enterprise where it is as efficient as in agriculture. He goes back to the origin of democracy, to the small property owners. Big industries should be operated as public corporations without government.

Modern capitalism is to be replaced by the public corporation. Here he is fuzzy. Then he says, strengthen organizations which are rivals of the government or prevent the government from monopolizing power. He gives the New Deal a high grade, not because it solved the economic problem—because it did not do that—but because it strengthened democracy in labor and farm organizations, and such. He says that criticism of the New Deal is that it has no plan. He says that the people said No plan, and got a super plan. He is against that.

Those who are for super plans are budding Fascists, because the power is in the hands of a few. Corey is for the dispersal of power.

I do not know if Corey's remedy (public corporations) has done much in the way of giving us a program of reconstruction. But I am taken with his ideas: power formation and democracy's goal of the dispersal of power.

THE
RUSSIAN
EXPERIENCE

PART SIX
Development

LECTURE 15
Changes in Capitalism and the Uniqueness of Russia and Its Mold

We went at length into the materialistic conception of history, class struggle, state and revolution, and imperialism and war. We have left out the structural changes in capitalism and the ultimate philosophy of Marx, or dialectic materialism. (Marxism sprang from Hegel.)

STRUCTURAL CHANGES IN CAPITALISM

Lenin's theory of imperialism is based upon the structural change of capitalism. Monopoly capitalism engenders imperialism.

The structural changes in capitalism may be treated in two ways: (1) concrete and descriptive or (2) theoretical and analytical. Lenin, in his writing about imperialism, is concrete. He starts out with capitalism, competitive capitalism, and larger units win out over smaller units, and finally, the merger of large ones into one, which is taken under the sponsorship of the banks. That is the descriptive or concrete method.

Another structural change in capitalism is the periodic breakdown of the whole system called depressions or crises. This is a periodic breakdown.

There is another way of going at the same subject of structural changes of capitalism, and that is the theoretical way. The labor theory of value and surplus theory of value, the whole analytical economics—Marx developed it. You may be content with a description that uses commonsense concepts or the way labor and businessmen understand things, or you may delve into the theoretical side and develop theoretical concepts. When you finish the job you can neither prove nor disprove. It is impossible to establish by statistics whether labor is the sole source of income, et cetera. We know a struggle is going on: each economic class is struggling for a maximum share in the national income.

61

Labor struggles for a share, and so on. The question of the struggle is observable to the naked eye, and it is not necessary to plunge into Marxist abstraction to convince oneself that struggle exists, because you can see it with the naked eye. Labor's struggle for a maximum share of wages is its way of trying to gain what is its own, which otherwise would have gone to exploiters—a secondary consideration.

We know that economic classes struggle and that each group is trying to get the best for itself. Due to concrete phenomena today, I do not think it is necessary to delve into the economic theory of Marx, but rather to go into concrete material. (I did this after considering it for some time.) I will turn to the Russian Revolution, the proletariat, their problems, and such matters. In view of the urgency of time, we will not discuss the theoretical account of Marx. *We will turn to Russia.*

The first assertion which I make with regard to Russia is that of all the European countries, Russia was the easiest job for the left-wing Marxist to master. That was because Russian society in 1917 was a society which, for historical reasons, lacked entities of resistance. It meant the special susceptibility of Russia in 1917 to a successful seizure of power from the left.

The Russian ruling class was characterized by weaknesses and lack of effectiveness in action. The Russian ruling class (landowners and big industrialists) were especially lacking in an effective will to power. As far as appearances went, the ruling group resembled their opposite numbers in other countries only on the surface. They lacked what it takes to make a ruling class. They tended to be more of a bureaucratic aggregation. In other words, people carrying out orders of others—the aristocrats rather than a group of people capable of government of their own when the old government was smashed.

The factors in Russia's makeup which shaped the unfolding drama were:

1. The psychological deficiency of the old Russian ruling classes.

2. The absence of a middle class characteristic of Russia. The absence of a sufficient middle class to serve as a coherent to big business. Russia had a very thin layer of small businessmen.

3. The special position of the Russian peasant. He was not an individual proprietor of land. The Russian peasant owned a hut and primitive implements of agriculture. He did not own land as an individual proprietor, but owned it collectively. Private property was the property of the large landlords in 1917. The Russian peasant thus was against private property because the landlords owned the land.

4. Arguments of labor. On the eve of the Russian Revolution labor was a highly dynamic and concentrated group. The laborers worked in large factories. Three or four million Russian proletarians were strategically located—they were in the big cities. They were important way beyond their numbers. They were also important because of their ultrarevolutionary psychology, and

they had it because under the old regime they had not been allowed to unionize. Russian factory labor was strategically placed and exposed to the full ravages of capitalism that prematurely reached the stage of monopoly capitalism and was wholly unchecked.

5. The role of the Russian intellectuals. There was no country in Europe in which the intellectuals as a class were so much looked up to. Even the Russian bureaucrats and industrialists, et cetera encountered revolutionary ideas, across the tables, in their children. The children made it quite uncomfortable for their elders and gave their elders a sense of inferiority. The landlords and industrialists found themselves beleaguered, since there was no middle class to look to for support; the peasants hated them and there was no comfort in their own homes, due to infiltration of revolutionary ideas in their children.

These were the factors that weakened conservatism in Russia. Conservatism was capable only of a weak kick. Western European conservatism was capable of a strong kick.

THE HISTORICAL MOLD OF RUSSIA

Government in Russia. The Russian state was an old state. According to Russian chronicles, the Russian state originated in the ninth century—year 862. It originated when the Russian tribes issued an invitation to the Scandinavians to come and rule over them, thus giving the new rulers the nicest mandate to rule. I doubt if this affair occurred so peacefully. The Scandinavians were sea-roving and fierce. By the end of the tenth century there had taken place a complete amalgamation of the Scandinavian pirates and the Russian tribes. You can tell this by the names—Slavic names. There was a fusion of an alien military aristocracy with an indigenous people.

Nature of the state. It was grouped around the city of Kiev. It was the capital of the first Russian state on the river Dnieper. The river flows to the Black Sea and is an artery of commercial traffic from the north of Europe to the only part of the European world that is a classical civilization—Constantinople (the southeastern corner of Europe; the Byzantine Empire).[1] There was commercial exchange between the north of Europe and the last remains of classical civilization. The Russians were a cross of pirates and merchants. Kiev was a commercial metropolis, and around it were subsidiary cities.

Internal order of the state. A certain kind of federation of city-states; Kiev was the center. Each city-state was headed by a prince. There was a group of princes, and they were all blood relations and ruled in the cities, but they were migratory princes and not permanently settled. They were promoted from a

1. The rest of Europe was in the dark days of the Middle Ages.

less significant town to a more important one when death knocked someone out. This really amounted to seniority. The princes were migratory and only temporarily situated.

Structure of the population of cities. The prince would have a small private army. The soldiers were his fellow warriors who were loyal to him. The cities were not military settlements. The army was small. Most important in the city were the merchants. (Trade in furs and honey was vital.) Merchants carried articles of commerce for Russia and were the middlemen for Scandinavia. They even carried to Constantinople. The plebeians were the artisans, laborers, and smaller merchants. Under the political constitution of early Russia you had something like a democracy.

A prince with his soldiers was not important, because he was migratory. It was the next step that he was looking to. The patriarchy had influence over the prince and the government—it also had a popular assembly. This was a democratic check on the prince and the merchant in the patriarchy. Russia was culturally far in advance of western Europe. This was due to its taking its culture from the Byzantine. It was Christianized in the year 990 and then the Russians studied Greek. There was an influence from the Greeks in the seventh and eighth centuries. In the twelfth century there existed something like a public school system in Kiev.

The whole thing was based upon free access to Byzantium, and that, in turn, was based upon the control of the lower reaches of the river. All that came to an end in the twelfth century, when there was a new invasion from Asia by the nomadic hordes, who did not understand the advantage of exacting tribute. They destroyed the economic system. They began to attack Russian cities just for plunder. Then there was a mass migration from the middle Dnieper toward the northern woods, where the people were out of reach of the marauders. That is how Moscow came to be founded. Moscow is between the two rivers, the Oka and the Volga. So there is a new Russia that springs into existence in the twelfth and thirteenth centuries. At the time of the new Russia, the economic basis was different—a Russia thrown back upon agriculture and a self-sufficient economy. It was also a Russia that lost its political freedom because it had to handle difficult problems due to the emerging premium on the leader—they all looked to him. In Kiev, the Russian prince was not so much. In northern Moscow, the Russian prince became more important. He was the organizer of economic life and the chief of police, the owner of land, and he gave land out as well. He was the lord of a large manor.

From a free commercial community, political freedom, you have now a magnified manor and the prince as the landlord and owner. There is the strengthening of the prince to the exclusion of all else.

The Tartars came in the thirteenth century and conquered the Russians, because the princes could not agree. Each hoped the Tartar wave would bypass him—they would not fight until they had to. The Tartars were moderate rulers, not destroyers. They were a final consciousness; they did not care to interfere with the Russian religion. The Tartars were businessmen; they wanted tribute. Under the Tartars, Russian life became disarmed as a subject nation does. Those in front were the intriguers. The princes of Moscow made their way to the top by knowing how to bribe, et cetera. The princes had the art of Laval[2] but they did not have his meanness. The princes strengthened nationalism. They were looked to as effective interceders between the Russian people and what was otherwise the unbearable consequence of conquerors.

LECTURE 16
The Background of the Russian
Revolution: The Russian State

In discussing the Russian program I will try to account for the Russian Revolution. I will give a bird's-eye view of the development of the state. The first Russian state was grouped around the city of Kiev. It was largely commercial. The second Russian state was grouped around Moscow. It sprang into existence during the twelfth and thirteenth centuries and its nature was agricultural. It was based on a self-sufficient economy. That altered the nature of the Russian community: a community representing a political partnership of prince, merchant, patriarchy, and the people. Now the community was based on the principle of aristocratic rule. A prince now became everything; he was military chieftain and economic enterpriser; he owned the land and allotted it to his followers. In the thirteenth century all of Russia was conquered and subjected by the Tartars—the western wing of the Mongol Empire. That had a coarsening effect on the community. From a cultured community Russia lapsed back to a low state of culture. Russia's national life in the spiritual field centered in the Church, the Greek Orthodox Church. This is the period of the rise to power of the princely house of Moscow. At first Moscow was small, but there was a succession of princes of Moscow who were skillful people in lobbying. In the end, with the aid of the Tartars, to whom they made themselves useful, the Moscow prince managed to annex other princes' lands. There was a gathering of land. The prince of Moscow became the grand prince of all other princes, yet under the rule of the Tartars. He became that not only by intrigue, but by popular will also. The Church had to be led by someone and that was the grand prince of Moscow. In the sixteenth century Russia emerged as an independent kingdom (it threw off the Tartars), but the structure is a monarchical structure.

2. Pierre Laval (1883-1945), French statesman prominent in international affairs in the 1930s. As an officer in the Vichy government, he advocated collaboration with Germany during World War II.

There was nothing in society that wanted independence. The grand prince—the czar—was everything. Other princes shaped themselves to the czar.

The boyars were descendants of the minor princes whose principalities the grand prince had taken over. Some were really superior to the grand prince, but they were different from the barons in England who forced the Magna Charta from the king: the barons in England got vital concessions from their own king. But the Russian boyars, as far as external position was concerned, resembled the barons of England—only the phenomenon was different. They were servile; they would intrigue but would not club together to force political concessions from the czar. They were not a political class and did not aspire to place men in government. The boyars continued to the end of the sixteenth century, when the old dynasty came to an end. The czar of Russia was Ivan IV, who ruled with an iron hand and beheaded the boyars.

By the end of the sixteenth century the old dynasty came to an end and the new ruler has since had an opera named for him.[1] The period 1598–1613 was a period of troubles and anarchy. Russia was suffering from anarchy because there was no legitimate ruler. The old house had died out. There was not enough political capacity in the aristocracy to build up a government. The aristocracy did nominate a new czar, but it did not support him. Anarchy ended by a national uprising led by the Church. The Russians expelled the foreign enemy and elected a new dynasty—the Romanov dynasty—that reigned for three centuries. They were related to the old dynasty by marriage. During the first half-century of the reign of the Romanovs the government was weak; you could say that here was a chance for the aristocracy to strengthen themselves, but they did not, because it was not in them and because they were busy trying to fasten a yoke on the peasants.

TO SHOW RUSSIA TOPSY-TURVY

The institution of serfdom in England ended in the fourteenth century. In Russia the peasants were free until the sixteenth century and then they became serfs, attached to the land. Until the end of the sixteenth century the peasant was permitted to change from one landlord to another. Now the landlords began to enjoy an attached labor force. So the landlords were busy controlling serfs. Throughout the seventeenth and eighteenth centuries we find the monarchy becoming stronger and stronger but encountering opposition. At the end of the seventeenth century the Russian ruler was Peter the Great, who decided to westernize Russia. Sweden blocked Russian ambition, so Russia had to become militarized in a modern sense. Peter the Great decided Russia was too backward and Russian life in general needed modernization. Peter

1. Czar Boris Godunov, the subject of a play by Pushkin and an opera by Moussorgsky based on the play, reigned 1598-1605.

took Holland for his model. He had learned the ship trade there and brought it back to Russia. He did not just change the external in Russia, but he was a cultural revolutionist. He liked to decide on Russian customs, and he was offered no opposition because of the tradition of nonresistance to the monarch. That came from the Byzantine Empire and from Russian history, because the Russians had to stand behind the monarch to free themselves from the Tartars. Thus you have the imprint of nonresistance to the monarch and the absence of any share in political power with the monarch. That continued into the eighteenth century during the reign of Catherine the Great (a German princess), who dethroned her husband and became the ruler. The guards helped to put her on the throne. She gave the nobility a chance to be like the German nobles. She did organize them into provincial assemblies. Here again they did not take advantage of the chance. The provincial assemblies became nonpolitical. Society became one of mutual aid and entertainment. That shows the historical mold of Russian nobility. It was nonpolitical.

In the fight against Napoleon and the great war of 1812, Russia defeated Napoleon and followed the retreating general to western Europe. Many of the Russian army officers in the whole period of fifteen to twenty years became acquainted with the Western order of things and ideas. Some came back inspired with the political order. The first revolution sprang up in the officers and culminated in 1825 in the famous rebellion, the *December Rebellion.* All were officers of the guard. There was political confusion. The czar was out of the picture in 1825. Officially he had died, but there was reason to believe he had wanted to abdicate and become a monk. He had a heavy sin on himself: he had helped to kill his father, Paul. There is reason to believe he put a hoax over on the people and did not die but went to a monastery. His brother Constantine had some of the traits of his father but said that he would not be czar. It is believed that he wanted to be urged to be czar. Nicholas, another brother, proclaimed himself as czar. Officers ordered regiments to the square; they said they were for Constantine. They said tell the men to yell "Long live Constantine and the Constitution." Nicholas had them shot. He suppressed the first revolution. The first revolution was a nobles' revolution.

After that, in 1825–56, it was black in Russia under Nicholas. Russian students were not allowed to travel abroad unless they had special permission. Pushkin at the time was a great poet and quite fruitful; he was exiled for a time.[2] It was a period of great cultural development up, under the nobility. An aristocratic culture but democratic, it had a populistic bent. The nobility had a sense of guilt because they used the peasants, and this impelled them to idealize the peasants. The village communes (the self-governing commune was a *mir*) attracted the attention of a German who wrote a book and told of them, saying it was a socialistic institution among the peasants. The nobility took it up and cherished it.

2. He was exiled from the capital, 1820-27.

In the middle of the nineteenth century, 1825–53, Russia was the greatest European continental power. Nicholas I saw to that. In 1848, the Hungarians rebelled along with the rest of Europe, and the Hungarian Revolution was suppressed by the Russian army. Nicholas sent the army to help his fellow emperor (from Austria). Then the Hungarians began to bear a grudge against Russia.

In 1853 Russia went to war against the alliance of France, Great Britain, and Turkey. Sardinia took a hand in that too. War took place in the Crimea, around Sevastopol, for three years. The Turks, French, and British besieged Sevastopol. Russia lost the war because she had no railroads. Russia needed railroads, needed to be modernized, and needed a change in reign too. Nicholas took poison. He could not stand the humiliation of being a defeated monarch. His son Alexander II became ruler. He was a liberal and a humanitarian. He emancipated the serfs in 1861—they were freed. He instituted governmental changes, reforms in courts, and municipal and county self-government. The reforms had to be crowned with a written constitution, but that was delayed. The bureaucrats were the top of the nobility. It all culminated in March 1881, when the emperor was assassinated. By that time the liberal movement, composed of professors and journalists, molded it and demanded that the Russian regime be altered along democratic and parliamentary lines. The main supporters of the demand were the intellectuals of Russia. They included a few of the nobility. On the whole, the Russian nobility chose to continue its old role of cleaving to the monarchy. They were officeholders and owned land; so they continued to the end of the nineteenth century. The government was pitted against the public opinion of Russia, and the extreme left of public opinion was the revolutionary movement. It consisted of not too many people, but they were bold—Russian students mainly. In 1905 a general strike hit Russia—a railroad strike. Everything stopped. It was a demonstration of the people demanding that a constitutional change be given to them. In October 1905, there was an official grant from the emperor.[3] It was not meant to be permanent; it was thought to quell the revolutionary movement. Seven weeks later the government started to take it back. The government diverted discontent from itself and placed it on the Jews. So the revolution was suppressed.

The ruling class of Russia, the Russian landowners and industrialists, who had no policy of their own, were just a hand behind the monarchy. They showed no willingness to act as a political class—not that individuals lacked physical courage, but they lacked political talent. They never thought of themselves as a political entity.

The revolution was suppressed and Russia had seven or eight years of prosperity. Then there was a great war—World War I—and Russia played a self-

3. In the October Manifesto, October 30, the czar granted civil liberties and a democratically elected duma.

sacrificing role. Part of the Russian army was in Germany; it was a disaster for Russia.

In the early months of 1917 the czar was obliged to abdicate. Then there was a period of six months of pulling and tugging and of uncertainty. It ended with the seizure of the government in October 1917 by the Bolsheviks. Then we saw civil war in Russia. It was a war of counterrevolutionists against the government. They had no political program or talent, so while they came within a short distance of capturing Moscow without a program, they collapsed. Here again, the collapse of the Russian White movement, or counterrevolution collapse, goes back to history. The nobility had no schooling in political action.

LECTURE 17
Russian Cities, Russian Industry and the Business Class, Religious Change

The influence which conditioned the Russian ruling class was the landed nobility. The history of the Russian state is of a government that was conducive to developing a nonpolitical attitude. It made the ruling class look upon itself as servants. It did not have the psychological attitudes or attributes of a ruling class. It fitted itself into the aristocracy and was dependent upon the aristocracy. The ruling class did not have the ability to create government in 1917. The Russian ruling class lacked a genuine gift for politics or for ruling the country. It was not able to build a new government.

The other privileged class in Russia was big business. Its historical background was just the same as the Russian aristocracy. Although on the surface it resembled the bankers and industrialists of western Europe, it was essentially something else. What was lacking was that the industrialists were not able to strike out for themselves.

Early Russia, grouped around Kiev, was commercial. The Russia of Moscow was agricultural, with no towns. Russia missed the stage of the medieval municipality. The medieval cities were the cradle of the middle class. The middle class started on a small scale in the guilds. It got various rights, and by and by developed into bigger business. The guilds and municipalities were the incubators of modern capitalism. Once a country goes through that development it is a country with evolution. In the guilds the middle class learned how to fight for interests, how to bargain until the French Revolution of 1789 made bigger demands. That, in western Europe, was the development of the middle class. The middle class acquires certain capabilities and propensities; it stands and governs itself and fights for its interests. The middle class cashed in on that during the end of the eighteenth century and the beginning of the nineteenth.

Russia missed that whole development. The cities in Russia were but residences of the governors—administrative centers. Russian cities were different from western European cities. There were two cities that were exceptions in the Baltic neighborhood. They did not belong to the Muscovite state until the sixteenth century. They were Novgorod and Pskov. They were the exception to the rule. Before they were taken by Russia they resembled the medieval cities. They were cradles of democracy but were obliterated in the sixteenth century by the czars.

The medieval self-governing cities were missing from Russia. There was little industry in Russia. For a long time the demand of the Russians for manufactured articles was ministered to by the peasant artisans. Villages manufactured things. The handicrafts of Russia were plied by the peasants during the winter. In the cities there were administrative officials, the garrison and officers, and a very few merchants who ministered to the people in the city. This was true down to 1700, to the time of Peter the Great. For his ideas he needed industries. Since he was a great admirer and imitator of western Europe, especially of Holland, he thought he would import mercantilism. Peter the Great thought he would import the mercantilistic setup into Russia, but he was disappointed. There was an absence of humans to serve as merchant-capitalist partners. He gave privileges to induce merchants to establish factories and the like. He did not tax them and gave them serf labor to make it easier. He attached villages under serfdom to a particular plant or factory so that they did not need to worry if there would be a sufficient labor supply. He took the products so that the merchant-capitalist did not need to worry about the market. Factories were established, but they were inefficient and passive. Russian mercantilism, instead of being a partnership of the government and the merchant, was a state mercantilism. Really industrial bureaucrats, the merchants took privileges, but they did not show initiative and energy. It was state mercantilism, and so it continued for a long time.

Thus Russian industry was started. A state-fostered industrial system, state-guaranteed market, labor, and profits. It was a very inefficient industrial system, a hothouse growth. This was the situation in the middle of the nineteenth century. On one hand there were large capitalistic factories—capitalistic in form and profits, but lacking the spirit of drive and energy. On the other hand, there were several million peasants in handicrafts. They worked for themselves and had initiative. They held their own against the factories. By 1860 the peasants had encroached upon the factories.

That is the background of Russian capitalism. However, it began to change. In the Crimean War, 1853–56, it began to change when Russia was defeated largely because of her lack of transportation. Then began a period of railroad-building, from 1856 on. Moscow was the heart of the railroads. They radiated from Moscow. By 1875 Russia was covered with a network of railroads which, for the first time, created an internal market for factories. Railroads were built for strategic reasons, so the army could be transported, and also so that Russia might carry surplus grain to western Europe.

As a by-product of the railroad-building, you had the development of an internal market. Russian textile manufacturers no longer needed the demand guaranteed by government. By and by factories realized the advantage and began to press it. By 1870, big industry was no longer held back; there was a private market. Thus big industry gave the peasant artisans a run for their money. They were put down by big industry. Even so, big industry was not freed from government tutelage. Russia went to the tariff protection system. The first tariff bill was drafted by a Russian chemist. He gave Russia a tariff system that smothered it rather than helped it. But still the factories continued to grow. Russian industry continued to be encouraged and supported by the government. There began a rapid evolution toward trusts in a monopoly form. An example is the sugar industry. It discovered that it had overextended and prices fell and it was in no position to organize a private trust. So the government came to its aid and the result was that the price of sugar was so high it was out of reach of the masses.

That was the industrial system which was based upon high protection and a high degree of dependence upon the government.

In order to put together a business organization, it would take sometimes two or three years in lobbying. Permission went to the people who knew how to lobby. That is an important factor—this extreme dependence upon the government for profit and the denial of freedom to move without government permission. The Russian government is a heavy hand upon business and that has consequences in psychologically shaping business.

In the showdown, the lobbyist was not a good scrapper. He was a good lobbyist but not a scrapper like Ford.[1] Thus you had the effect of government patronage in business. The successful man was not one endowed with tooth and claw, but a smoothie businessman. That is why when the downfall occurred in Russia in the 1900s, they sat back and did nothing. They were not of fighting stock. The government system had prevented the leaders of business from being fighting men.

Another reason why Russian business showed a lack of resistance was because it was too highly concentrated and because of abnormal development. In western European cities there was normal development; the concerns were large, but

1. Henry Ford (1863-1947), American automobile manufacturer universally identified as the creator of mass production through innovative use of the assembly line.

they were shielded on the side of business of lesser size. An example is Germany, which had seven times as many small and medium-sized concerns as were found in Russia. Small concerns are a proving ground for business leadership. Another use of medium and small businesses was that they served as a cover, a flank of big business. In Russia the flanks of big business were exposed. Also, the Russian business system did not profit from this kind of social covering. The Russian peasants owned land collectively. Business is dependent on private property, and the peasants hated it. The peasants themselves had no interest at that time in private property.

The historical background of the business class in Russia was one that was shaped for dependence on the government.

Labor relations. The government did not allow trade unions to exist. This was pleasant for the large Russian employer. The life of the Russian businessman was ideal. In the long run it exposed the business system to destructive attack from the left. Russian businessmen were not toughened like the American businessmen who fight. A strike or lockout is a good thing for businessmen because it makes them strong. Unionism, when it exists, becomes practical and conservative and interested in wages, hours, and the like. In Russia, by preventing unionism, business was immediately favored; but in the long run it was hurt. Also, Russian labor was prevented from developing conservative traits.

Russian businesses were given improper conditioning. Business was over-pampered.

Another development. There was a reformation in the religious sphere—a religious struggle. In England and Holland and other countries, when religion changes it is a movement of the middle class reformers in pursuit of their right to religious freedom and to profess their own faith; they develop a capacity for political action. They unite to gain religious freedom and fight for it—thus the capacity to stand together and enforce rights. They become a political class. Their fight for their religion shapes them into a political class. This was a byproduct of the sixteenth and seventeenth centuries, the shaping of the middle class into a political entity.

Russia did not have that; there was no religious reformation. There was one in name only at the end of the seventeenth century when books on religion were revised. It was done by a patriot of the Russian Church. That aroused the opposition of the Russians, who thought it was the work of the devil. The result was a split in the Church. There were divisions—secessionists, or Old Believers, who did not fight it out; they accepted, for their model, nonresistance. They went into the woods and tried to live by themselves. They were taken by the government; the soldiers went into the churches and burned. Out of such an experience you do not develop the Scotch Calvinist type of fighter—a fighter who could have prevented communism in Russia.

LECTURE 18
Why Revolution in Russia?

BACKGROUND OF THE RUSSIAN REVOLUTION

I will read parts of a paper I gave in 1919. The Russian Revolution then was two years old. The paper was written in October and given in December 1919. The White armies were close to Moscow. It looked as though the Soviet regime would be liquidated. The leaders feared for their regime. The number one leader was Lenin, and Trotsky was number two. Lenin said, We will probably be defeated, but when we make an exit we will bang the door so the whole capitalistic world will feel it. But he did not need to bang the door, because they won. It was also a time of strong anti-Red hysteria in the United States. The United States district attorney arrested Reds; he wanted to be presidential timber.

A treatment of the subject of the background of the Russian Revolution, written in the midst of the crisis when its fate was in the balance, was "Bolshevism and Democracy," in the American Sociological Society volume 14 (1919). I will read this article to give the contemporary atmosphere in 1919.[1] It shows the anti-Red hysteria and fear of Bolshevism coming to the United States, and the exaggeration of small groups of revolutionary leaders and members which caused anti-Red emotion to be inflamed. There is something like this now—an antilabor emotion.

Why did the revolution come to Russia? Why did Russia go communistic? That is a pertinent intellectual problem.

There is the landed gentry in Russia, whose history is interwoven with the Russian state. Then I talked about the capitalists and the middle class. The Russian capitalist and middle class were weak, anemic, and artificial.

The Russian peasantry was different from the west-European peasantry. In western Europe, peasants were freed in the early part of the nineteenth century. In France, the French Revolution did it. The peasants were emancipated and developed into peasant proprietors. In England, personal freedom was obtained several centuries before. In Russia, the peasants were hit by the Revolution of 1917, not as owners of property held as individuals, but of land they owned collectively. Private land was in the estates of the landlords.

Russian history is upside down. The peasants in western countries were first serfs and then freed. In Russia the peasants were free until as late as the sixteenth century. They were allowed to change landlords. They were subject to

1. Professor Perlman read his article, "Bolshevism and Democracy," which appeared in *The Problem of Democracy*, Publications of the American Sociological Society, vol. 14 (Chicago: University of Chicago Press, 1920), pp. 216-25. See Appendix C.

free labor contract. The changing of masters took place on St. George's Day. Gradually the peasants were attached to the land. Toward the end of the sixteenth century was the beginning of Russian serfdom. Two kinds of serfs existed: those owned by the private landlord and those state peasants owned directly by the czar. The peasants were rebellious; they ran away and settled on the frontier. The Cossacks, for instance, ran away and organized a free republic. They were engaged in wars and got booty. They especially liked to fight the Turks, and they also fought the Moscow government. The serfs who ran away formed free voting communities. More and more, those who stayed at home became slaves, but they were unruly. Then the idea of collective responsibility arose. The whole village was considered a tribute-paying entity. That held whether the peasants were state or private, and that was the village commune, which was put across by fiscal necessity and control. Its purpose was to control the peasants in order to deliver labor and other produce. Collective responsibility was put upon them, so that the village was treated as a village. It followed that the village must have a certain amount of economic government. Land was administered by the village. Land was in two parts, one part for the landlord and the other part for the peasants for their own subsistence. The latter part came to the village as a chunk. The village would assign strips of land to families, and the allotment was based on the number to be fed in a family. The village was the collective administrator of that part of the land that was assigned to the peasants for their own use and that thus established its own self government—the *mir*—a system of collective possession of land and collective administration of the allotment of the land. The village commune with a socialist pattern of economy. Once in ten years or twelve there was a general reshuffling in order to equalize opportunity to the families. No family was allowed to hang on to a strip indefinitely. During the shuffling, adjustments were made according to the size of the family. Those with more children were given more strips of land. That came into existence in the sixteenth and seventeenth centuries, and it came in gradually and under serfdom. There was economic self-government, but without ownership.

Then there was the emancipation of the peasants, forced upon the state by the defeat in the Crimean War and the rising unrest of the peasants. By 1886–87 the emancipation of the peasants was in the cards; the plan was studied and worked out by the government. The occupant of the throne was Alexander II, who was more liberal than his father. He was known as the Czar Liberator. Peasants asked how they were to be freed. Should they be freed like the peasants in the West—cut loose landless (go to the cities and become the proletariat)? The government wanted to head off proletarianism among the peasants, because that would head off revolution. So the idea was to keep the commune and transfer to the commune the prerogatives of the family held by the landlord, and to regard the commune as the collective owner of land held by the peasants. It was ownership at a price. The government treated all land as the

private property of the landlords; that part that went to the peasants had to
be paid for. The peasants had no money, so the government was the intermediary. Government commissions set a price, and the government issued bonds
and they were given to the landlords to compensate for their lost title to lands.
That meant the government acted as a bank and extended credit to the newly
established communes as corporate owners of land. The government established a forty-nine-year mortgage plan. Each year the commune was to turn
over to the government a certain amount of money. The original price of land
was too high, because the commission was largely landlords. Thus there was
involved a large indebtedness of the peasants when they were freed, as well as
taxes. The main burden fell upon the peasants.

LECTURE 19
The Russian Peasants

We took up social groups in Russia as units of social action in light of action
and in light of the past. The landed gentry, the capitalist class, and now the
peasantry. The peasantry was different in Russia in 1917, and even today it is
marked off from other countries of the West and of Europe in the sense of
being a landowning class. In old Russia, the form of landownership was collective ownership—the village was a collective entity. Today Russia is even
more collective. There was the periodic allotment of land and collectivism was
expressed in the concerted type of agriculture. One Russian peasant operated
in concert with other peasants. Agricultural operations had to proceed in uni-
son because of certain rights or claims all the families had. After the harvest
season the whole village turned cattle out onto the land. A single peasant
could not say "I am going to run my agriculture different from the rest." Collectivism in the life of the peasants was first in the ownership of land and its
disposition, and second, in that while each family operated as a distinctive
unit it was at the same time in lockstep with the rest. That meant that the
mode of operation was traditional. One year out of three the land was allowed
to lie fallow. Strips of land a family had in a field that was fallow had to lie
fallow. Thus they could not move to an advanced agricultural system with a
crop rotation system.
    So then you have two aspects of collectivism in the old Russian village—land
ownership and families in lockstep.
    Now in Russia peasant life is far more collectivized. That is because produc-
tion has become collectivized. It is one economy where peasants are not individual enterprisers, but are really employees of a collective and paid on the
basis of hours of toil put in.

In Russia in 1917 the collective note was strong and private property was weak. Implements, cattle, and the like were not so very important; land was important. It was the major item of ownership, and if it were held by collectivists then you had a lack of agreement on private property in general. That is why the peasant did not respect private property, nor did he have much of a sense of guilt if he took something. The peasants are a class who had not gone through the school of private proprietorship.

One reason why Russian resistance to Germany was so successful and why they used the scorched earth policy was because they never had had much private property. Things were collectively owned; that is why the Russians could carry out the policy of scorched earth.

I refer you to the book I read by William L. Shirer, *Berlin Diary.*

The Russian Peasants on the Eve of the Revolution. The peasants were emancipated in 1861 as part of the land and they were not a landless peasantry. Part of the land was sold to peasant communes with the government acting as a financial intermediary and the communes were to make forty-nine payments—redemption payments. Before long the two items of payments, redemption plus taxes, became an unbearable burden, especially when the crops were bad. The burden on the village was good for the government. Villages were collectively responsible for payments. Before long the economic effects showed it to be bad. First the price of land charged to the peasants was too high. Another reason was that since the peasant was not an individual proprietor and since the strip he got depended on the size of his family, there was no reason to hold the family size down. The French peasant keeps the family size down so they do not have to divide the land up so much. Proprietary instinct and social status acted on the birth rate in France or on the peasantry who had individual proprietorship. Instead of holding down the family, Russia had the opposite inducements. The strips you got depended on the size of the family. The result was that population increased at a high rate and thus you had a vicious circle. The peasants felt themselves obliged to plow up the meadow or pasture lands for foodstuffs. The result of that was the shrinkage of cattle, less natural fertilizer, and thus impoverishment of the soil, necessitating the plowing up of more land. The peasants went downward.

There were a good many causes for the downward trend of the peasants: the commune itself was a cause. The collective arrangement is a cause because it deprived the peasant of obtaining new agricultural methods and held the family close. But the peasants liked the commune and never blamed it. They blamed the government and the landlords. The government was blamed for high payments. The government forced them to sell on the market what otherwise they would have used. Thus agricultural exports were really hunger exports. Then they cast an eye on the land that remained in the large estates. After emancipation landlords still owned 50 percent of the land, and the peasants cast an eye on that. Their ethical approach to the problem was that the Lord created the land and humans, and humans should cultivate. He who does not cultivate the land has no right to it. Thus, they were theologians. The landlords, in their eyes, had no right to the land. They knew the landlords had legal rights, but believed they had no moral right. Even as serfs they said to the landlords: "Sure we are yours, but the land is ours."

The cure-all that the peasants sought was to get hold of the land and abolish landlordism and extend the holdings of the village to the adjacent private estates.

For four or five decades the conditions of the peasantry kept getting worse and worse. There were famines which resulted in agrarian disorders. The peasants started the red rooster, setting fire to the landlords' dwellings and so forth.

By 1901 or 1902, the revolutionary parties succeeded in connecting up with the peasants. The revolutionary parties connected up with agrarian disorders. The peasants took a part in the revolutionary movement of 1905 and 1906. Their part was anarchical but they made themselves felt and the government was disappointed. The government had thought the commune would keep the peasant conservative and immune from revolutionary ideas. Now it saw that this was not happening. The commune was acting as a conductor of revolutionary ideas. When the government had mastered the revolutionary movement by 1906, it changed its attitude toward the communes. The government put thumbs down on the commune and encouraged individual proprietors. So there was the agrarian reform of the year 1906; the government devoted itself to breaking up the commune. Under the old form the peasant could not leave the commune unless two-thirds would agree to let him go (this was from 1861 to 1906). If the peasant wanted to go to the city to work he had to get a passport from the commune. The peasant stood toward the commune as he had toward the landlords in many ways. The peasants of energy and ability were the last ones the commune would let go. The efficient peasant was not permitted to quit the commune. But under the law of 1906, the government made it possible for the peasant to get out of the commune merely by filing an application. You could separate out. Then the question arose as to how much land should be given out as his share. In order to stimulate separation the government showed favor to the separatist. If the applicant had more land than he was entitled to in view of the size of his family—then he was permitted to hold it and was obliged to make payment of excess payment of the land, but at the price of 1861. Thus, you see the government favored the separatist. It scattered peasants from villages to the open land; it felt the villages were the center of revolutionary propaganda. Between 1906 and 1914 that was the policy of the government and a great deal was accomplished. One-twentieth or one-eighteenth did separate out. Their lot was none too sweet either. The government was on their side but there was one reason why the government

was so eager for each peasant to have his own farm. On the way from the land
back to the village, accidents happened. Then there was war, so the process of
the government breaking up the villages ended.

During the war Russian agriculture had its ups and downs. "Ups" were the
prices; "downs," the Russian army used the horses and manpower was used.
The military breakdown started in 1915 and the Revolution occurred in 1917—
the government fell and it was three months until the seizure of power by the
Soviets.

In 1917 one of the first acts of the new government—which was headed by
Lenin—was the declaration that all land was national property. This was
theoretical—a gesture. The practical or actual case was that the peasants were
invited to help themselves to the land of the private estates. The landlords
were asked to move off, or if they stayed on they were treated as peasants.
The communes realized their aspirations 100 percent. All of the private estates
were merged into communal holdings of neighboring villages. The remarkable
thing was that there was little bloodshed. For example, two villages with an
estate between (in America there would be fights) found annexation peaceful.
They knew how to compromise. There were annexations in 1917 and 1918
and the peasant realized his life-long aspiration—the end of landlord owning.
To each family according to its needs—this idea reigned supreme (with some
reservations). The government kept some model estates—which later ceased to
be model estates.

That is why the peasants lined up behind the Reds—behind the communists
rather than the Whites. The Whites did not have enough political sense. The
Whites would string up villagers and restore estates.

However, the peasants did pick bones with the new government. They were
disillusioned with it and the favor of getting land. When the counter-revolutionary army upset the land arrangements, then the peasants forgot their
grievances against the new government, because the old government would
push them back to the old system.

When, in 1920, the counter-revolutionary army was defeated the peasants
rebelled against the new government because of requisitions and the like. Then
there were rebellions and the new government changed its policy and you got
a New Economic Policy (NEP). What was the NEP? Journals—papers—say it
was old capitalism. I thought at the time it was not that but a concession to
the peasants. The peasants turned in one portion of their crops and the rest
was free. So from 1922 to 1929, in seven or eight years the Russian peasants
were relatively well off. They had all the land they wanted and at the same
time were permitted to conduct their own affairs. Russian agriculture recov-
ered quickly. It was a great lifesaver for the Russian people.

If you conduct radical change, pick an agricultural country because it can absorb shocks. The population in cities, while bungling with the industrial system, can be fed by the villages.

Communism is an advanced model of revolution. It is only a backward country with a large peasant class that can afford the luxury of a revolution. Look for backward agricultural countries for experimental grounds for social organization, because they can stand shocks.

LECTURE 20
The Russian Working Class

SOCIAL FORCES IN RUSSIA ON THE EVE OF REVOLUTION, 1917

Last time I discussed the state of the peasantry and its attitude. Now I will discuss the working class, the wage-earning class. The Russian working class was predominantly factory workers; that goes back to the nature of Russian industry. There were two types of industry in Russia: the village handicrafts (three or four million peasants engaged in these in their own villages), and agriculture. They ministered to the moderate wants of great masses of people, providing such items as hardware and felt boots. In western Europe, what four million peasants were doing had been for many centuries carried on in cities by the urban class. When England was visited by the Industrial Revolution (the year was 1800) there was a class of artisans who lived in the cities—a class of artisans who had many generations of urban life behind it. They were descended from the guilds. There was a class of journeymen who organized into trade unions as early as the second part of the seventeenth century. So, in 1800, when the Industrial Revolution was in full swing in England, there was a society with two working classes. One had long roots in urban life, descended from the guilds—the wage earners in trade societies who bargained with employers (even though, under the law, their status was uncertain). Especially in 1800 when Parliament passed an anticombination law. It was a precarious life, but still they existed and functioned because the meshes of the British legal net were wide and could not catch many of the small fish. That was England in 1800—a large artisan class organized in unions, subject to being swooped down upon, but managing. It was an artisan class with a long tradition of self-organization dating back to the guilds and even as trade unions dating back to the seventeenth century. They had acquired the ability to organize and protect their interests and they knew how to duck whenever the law came looking for them.

A different class really were the peasants in the factories (they came to work in cotton mills and the like) who had no habits or experience in collective action and had not acquired trade union experience.

The artisans in southern England looked after their economic interests and were quite well educated and so were interested in politics. They knew the political ropes, but it was not until two more generations had elapsed before they got the franchise. They knew some Parliament members and some masters were political radicals. Francis Place was a master tailor, but in reality he was a politician for the people. Due to his efforts, an anticombination law was not renewed in 1825. The artisan class in England was anything but helpless. They were quite at home.

It was the factory class of workers who were helpless. They were uprooted from villages and housed in barracks in cities like Manchester. They were the real proletariat and had no friends. They constituted the revolutionary element in England at that time. They broke the machines and equipment. That was the English situation in 1800.

The Russia of 1917 was similar insofar as the working class was concerned. Where was the counterpart of the London artisans of 1800 and 1825? The peasants in villages knew crafts but they were scattered and had no experience in organizing. Russia lacked that sturdy class of artisans which in England had played a political role and where labor found political expression. In Russia this was out of the picture. Russia had no counterpart of the Manchester group of 1800. In the big Russian factories you had a factory proletariat pretty much like the proletariat in England in Manchester, 1800. Conditions were crowded and congested, there were low wages, the workers were poorly housed and had no trade unions. The Russians were governed by bureaucracies and secret police who were alert to the danger of trade unions. It was, therefore, difficult for trade unions to survive. The unions were secret, what few there were. The Russian factory worker in 1910 was unprotected. Trade unionism was prohibited and the prohibition enforced. It was not like England where the union was in court as a combination—but this did not even happen to many. There was a difference between the Russian proletariat in 1910 and the British of 1800.

The British working class of 1910 was a mighty trade union movement with two million members. The key industries were unionized; trade agreements were in use; and there were industrial boards. There was a strong trade union organization and it was influential, acting as a shield for its membership. They also had labor legislation with minimum wage laws.

In Russia in 1910-17, the British artisan counterpart was the peasant in the village. The factory proletariat of 1917 was the counterpart to the British proletariat in 1800.

Revolution came to Russia at a time when Russian labor had not yet managed to build up any protective institutions. In England in 1910 and 1917, the main leadership of labor was that which had risen from the ranks. The 1912 strike found Parliament enacting a law to grant the demand for minimum wages. Behind this action was the leader, a Scotch miner, Robert Smillie. England had a leadership schooled in the school of trade unionism that looked after job interests. Smillie was also a Socialist, but he was primarily a trade union leader.

In Russia, who were the leaders of the workers when they rebelled? In St. Petersburg (the most important industrial city in Russia at the time) a strike movement occurred in the winter of 1894-95. The most important leader in the strike movement was Lenin. It was a revolutionary leadership from amongst the intellectuals of Russia. Lenin came from the lower nobility. Leadership came from the intellectuals. What drew Lenin into the strike movement of 1894-95? It was his conviction that the factory proletariat was destined by history to bring in socialism—communism. Lenin's relations to the working people were absolutely honest. He really cared for them. He was interested in the concrete conditions of labor. He was a first-class researcher and investigator. This fact shows in the leaflets he composed and spread among the workers. One was *Factory Fines.* There were fines on workers for tardiness, poor work, et cetera. At the same time there was a difference between Smillie and Lenin. Lenin was primarily interested because labor could be a revolutionary vehicle. He was interested in the concrete—the control of the strike movement from the standpoint of his own party. He believed in party-controlled unions. That is the important thing. Factory workers in Russia were living under the same conditions as the English had about seventy-five years earlier. In 1907 the Leningrad (Petrograd) census was taken and it was found that two-thirds never had cut their ties with their native villages. Later on these ties were to their advantage (in 1917 and 1918) because there was nothing to eat in Leningrad and the people had to go back to the villages. This was another reason why Russia could weather the Revolution without the workers stopping. When production practically stopped it did not mean mass starvation because the factory workers could go back to their own villages. They were welcomed in their own villages because they now possessed certain skills.

A country that is not very developed industrially is better off in a revolutionary period than a highly developed country because a developed country

has a large population in the cities. In the community Russia possessed a tie
between workers and villages which helped the workers during the critical
period after the Revolution.

But this tie before the Revolution shows another side. The factory workers
were still something of a migratory population. In winter the labor market
was flooded by peasants coming to the cities after the end of their agricultural work. Winter wages would take a dip; there was a summertime shortage
of labor in the cities because the workers would go back to the villages to
work—so summer wages went up. There were bad housing conditions in the
Russian factory centers due to the violent pulsation—fluctuations in the numbers of the working class. Of course, the government was to blame too. The
buildings put up were poorly constructed because of the uncertainty of steady
all-year-round occupancy. Thus, there existed great congestion and bad conditions for the workers. The Russian worker would say, "I'm occupying a corner
of such and such a room."

Some groups were better off. The skilled machinists who earned better wages
could live better, but then they were the upper crust. The bulk of the workers
were the Marxist tailor-made proletariat. Workers were not permitted to develop
protective institutions of their own or to bring forth leadership of their own.
Thus they were revolutionary. Leadership came from the outside, from the
revolutionary intellectuals.

The very locations of industries were controlled by the labor factor, low
wages, and such. That is why Moscow was an important manufacturing city.
It was the center of population. The region was thickly populated with peasants and there was a scarcity of land. Factories were located there because of
low wages. Coal had to be transported over a long distance from the south.
All of these circumstances account for the behavior of the Russian proletariat.
The German proletariat disappointed the Marxists.

Preceding the war of 1914,[1] there had been revolutionary activity. In the
First Revolution,[2] the proletariat was the revolutionary class. Even the half-
conservative papers talked of the heroic peasants. For a little while when
there was the written constitution (October 1905)[3] unions sprang into existence and grew like mushrooms. The brief existence of unions had showed a
trend toward trade unions. By 1907 they had been suppressed.[4] When the
Revolution again started up it was under the auspices of the intellectuals.

1. World War I.
2. "Bloody Sunday," January 22, 1905, was followed by strikes, peasant riots, armed
clashes—revolt.
3. The October Manifesto.
4. The dissolution of the second duma.

Then came World War I, and on the eve of war came another wave of strikes. Frenchmen came to visit Russians, who were embarrassed because everyone was on strike. With war came a wave of patriotism; the strikers went back to work. It was felt that the war could do Russian liberalism a great deal of good and that the Russian regime would be changed. The liberals in Russia acclaimed the war against Germany. The Western democracies disappointed them. They did not, after all, pressure the czar to make changes in the regime. In fact, they whitewashed the czar. The effect of the alliance—instead of causing the government to make concessions, it became more reactionary.

What happened to the working people during the war? It was a deplorable contrast when compared to the United States, England, and other countries. Elsewhere the labor movement came to be more acceptable. Even the German army looked on the trade unions as being more acceptable. In 1916 the German high command pressured big business to make some concessions to labor. Even in Germany labor received wider social and political concessions. This was not the case in Russia. Labor committees in Russia would function one day and be arrested the next. Wages were held down and the hours of labor and the intensity of labor increased. Workers were driven to increase their output and got no reward. Their condition—spiritual and material—during the war was getting steadily worse. If in 1906 and 1907 factory workers were tailor-made to Marxism, in 1916 and 1917 they were doubly so. That accounts for the Marxist-like behavior of the factory workers. Perhaps three and one-half million factory workers were highly concentrated and greatly dissatisfied. Any change would be better.[5]

5. Here analogy to the lot of the Chinese peasant might be called to attention—anything would be better than the present. The question might well be raised: Is it possible communism takes hold when conditions are so bad that *any change* is worth the gamble and risks entailed? The idea that it could not be any worse but might possibly be better—this is a simple theory but nevertheless one that might well be profound in its ramifications if pursued.

PART SEVEN
The
Revolutionary Outlook

LECTURE 21
The Role of the Intellectuals in the
Russian Revolution

THE ROLE OF THE INTELLECTUALS IN THE RUSSIAN
REVOLUTION AND THEIR BASIC PHILOSOPHIES

Looking at the role of the intellectual is difficult because it is not easy to define the term "intellectual." The intellectual is one who is interested in social and political movements. In Russia the origin of the intellectual was from among the nobility—at least the lower nobility. The nobility is a numerous class in Russia, including even the sons of the peasants and petty merchants who receive education. The role of the intellectuals of Russia can be contrasted with the intellectuals of the West.

Take, for instance, Germany—the revolutionary movement began under such intellectuals as Lassalle and Marx. They mapped out the course of the movement; they mapped out the roles groups were to play and the outcome. The remarkable thing about the intellectual diagnosis and forecast as far as the Western world is concerned was that it proved to be quite inadequate. Actual life proved to be superior to the intellectual ideas. The intellectuals proved to be inadequate prophets. Something arose in the countries to sidetrack or circle the revolutionary train. In such Western countries as the United States, England, Italy, and Germany, present reading exposes the programs and social philosophies of the intellectuals. You find the thing is dated. The programs in mind were not typical of life. It was a different situation in Russia. The course of the revolutionary leader was different in 1917-18 to 1922-23, the critical years of the revolutionary regime. Forecasts made by Lenin around 1902 and 1903 were fully fifteen to twenty years before the events occurred, and there

84

was a close correlation. In 1902 and 1903 Lenin sketched several phases of the Russian Revolution. When it broke out in 1917 and during the following years, it followed what Lenin had laid down. Why was it so? Must one draw conclusions that of all the intellectuals Lenin was the only clear-sighted one—or something else?

Background of the Revolution. An absence of centers of resistance to revolution in the form of historically developed classes—landed gentry and industrial classes ruling in name only. In the historical process they lacked political intent. The peasantry of Russia differed from that in the Western world. In the Western countries the revolutionary prophet overshot the mark. The intellectuals overshot the mark because they failed to display realism in the forces then hostile to revolution. In Russia, because she lacked centers of resistance, there was no chance to overshoot the mark. You forecast development and it does not take place because of resistance; but rather when resistance is at a minimum, the intellectual then has an advantage in his forecasting.

In Germany in 1890 it was taken for granted that labor leaders would be revolutionary—revolutionary Marxians. By 1890 the leaders professed contempt for labor trade unionism. In Germany in 1890 it was taken for granted that the leaders of the labor movement would be revolutionary. This was not the case as we saw later. Marxist intellectuals like Kautzky cast the German proletariat in the role of a revolutionary. Then trade unions arose and the proletariat played a different role which was not revolutionary. The trade union leadership they followed was a pattern preferred by trade agreements and the like. In Russia the intellectual revolutionaries who made the forecasts were the ones who put their own programs over. They had no rivals. Russian society was passive by nature. When the old regime collapsed the very forecasters of Revolution to come found themselves the only doers. In social movements we are all guessers; the best we can do is to develop rough notions. The Russian conditions were special. The prophets could pull strings and make the mathematics look right. Forecasts were justified by performance.

The Russian revolutionary intellectuals were not so farsighted. They were no more farsighted than the Germans, but they were fortunate because they could make forecasts come true. They could discard the clothes of the forecaster and don the clothes of the knight and slay the dragon that could hardly crawl. The other revolutionary intellectuals or leaders found their forecasts were affected by dragons which sidetracked everything.

When Lenin applied his analytical ability as a social statistician to the Western countries he was wrong. He thought that world revolution was at hand. He sent an army toward Poland and thought then there would be a social revolution of the peasants in Poland. He joined with General Gurploski. Lenin supported the general's military plan because he figured the peasants would arise and there would be a republic. The peasants flocked to the army and defeated the Russian army. Wherever else it was tried—Hungary, Bavaria—wherever revolutionary strategy was tried (that was satisfactory in Russia) it invariably failed and failed because the social structures of those countries were different from Russia's. There were powerful social groups that fought the revolutions. The social diagnosis of Lenin's worked in Russia, but not outside of Russia. He viewed the countries of Western Europe through his revolutionary dogma. Russia was a tailor-made heaven for revolutionary intellectuals.

REVOLUTIONARY THINKING IN RUSSIA

Revolutionary philosophies came in two classes: those that have an international intellectual horizon and those of a strictly national horizon. That runs through the Russian revolutionary movement—two kinds of thinkers and programs. One envisioned Russia as a part of the world—and they thought of world revolution—and the other of a national revolution. In the intellectual horizon the Russian Revolution enthroned two groups: those whose horizon was global—an intellectual horizon beyond Russian boundaries—and those whose horizon was limited to boundaries. This does not mean that those with a world horizon are the greater idealists. As a matter of fact, those with a Russian horizon, with regard of person, were greater and higher. The distinction was between a wider intellectual horizon and a narrower intellectual horizon. In the year 1918, after the October Revolution in December 1917, the power was in the hands of two parties—a coalition, a coalition of the party headed by Lenin and Trotsky (the Bolshevists), and the other the left wing of the Social Revolutionary Party. The Bolshevists were a faction of the Social Democratic Party. The Bolshevists understood the Russian Revolution which they put over. To them it was a stepping-stone to world revolution. They felt the Western world was ready for an anticapitalist revolution. A breach in capitalism in Russia could have meaning if it could serve as a world-wide revolution, and so they proposed to use the Russian Revolution as leverage for world-wide revolution. The revolution in Russia thus had to have a strong government—a dictatorship, a proletariat dictatorship. It was of use to a world-wide revolution; take Russia and use it on behalf of the world revolution. In order to do so, it was necessary to have a tie-up and a dictatorship to pick up and have a world revolution. An example here of world-revolution mindedness is a revolutionary program of a global horizon. Russia was to serve as a means to bring on world-wide revolution. The new government had its ups and downs. One was the refusal of the Western proletariat to follow in the footsteps of the Russian Revolution. This led to a drastic peace treaty—a treaty of Brest-Letovsk—and Germany got the Ukraine and the Lenin government was obliged to accept it. They said it was a temporary setback. One-third of the peasants were brought back under the yoke of the landlords and the German master. They were sorry to yield but not to do so would have created a catastrophe. They took it as a disastrous Bull Run. Later something else might be done; they took it and planned for a new revolutionary offensive.

Contrasted to this is the left wing of the Social Revolutionary party. It was an ally of the Lenin party in the October Revolution. It had a national intellectual horizon. Intellectuals were close to the village; Lenin and Trotsky were close to the urban dweller. The left wing of the Social Revolutionary party was emotionally close to the peasants. They were national minded. They, too, wished the Western proletariat well in putting over the revolution. They wished the French, British, and German proletariat would be successful in their own revolutions. But then the national-minded revolutionaries, while they wished the West well, saw no reason for sacrificing Russia to a world-wide revolutionary objective. They wished them well but did not wish to sacrifice the Russian peasants to help the Western revolutions. The treaty signed by Lenin, Brest-Litovsk, which turned over one-third of the peasants to Germany, was one they could not reconcile themselves to. It was a moral catastrophe. They could not accept it and felt compelled to fight it. So they opposed the treaty and wanted to declare war on Germany—to start a revolution, a liberating war to free the peasants of the Ukraine. They were shocked by their allies, the Bolshevik party. They could not see how the world-wide revolutionaries were so callous to their own people. They tried to change their allies' minds but could not do so. So they turned their guns on the allies. They began to embarrass the allies. First of all they assassinated the German minister in Moscow. This was embarrassing for the Russian government—for the Bolsheviks. The Lenin government was obliged to justify itself. It had to set up police to capture the terrorists. That started the whole thing off. Later on, one of the members of the party turned his guns on Lenin and Lenin was wounded.

My purpose is to give two kinds of revolutionary outlooks—one international and the other national. The people who killed the German ambassador and later tried to kill Lenin were not gangsters. They were sensitive to the condition of the peasants in the Ukraine.

The distinction now reappears—it reappeared much sooner than the present—the distinction between the world-wide horizon and the Russian horizon. It appeared in 1924 in the conflict between Stalin and Trotsky. Stalin said socialism was possible in one country. Trotsky was insisting that socialism is one country is impossible. Technology is for socialism and that is world-wide. Trotsky wished to work for world revolution. Stalin said, "I, too, am for world revolution, but under the circumstances, do what we can for Russia proper."

This is the contrast between world revolution and something you can do in one country. In Russia it reappeared without reproducing the ethical sensitiveness of those in 1918 who felt they had to kill the German ambassador because

of the peasants in the Ukraine. On the intellectual side the contrast is reproduced in 1924 between Stalin and Trotsky. It was a matter of fact because
Stalin would not discuss world-wide revolution; his was a do-first-things-first
attitude. Russia was at his feet and socialism was there at first.

The present is similar. The conflict of two ideas reappears in the present war
situation. It figures in discussions of what Russia will do if she wins over Germany. We say, watch Russia, she is out for world revolution. Watch out for
Bolshevism. Do so by not supporting Russia—fight just the Japs. Others say
that Russia is no longer an international conspiracy; it is a self-centered national state, so we can render aid to Russia without fear that after victory
Russia will turn around and try to spread the communistic system.

Today the issue is, Does Russia had a world-wide horizon or is she revolutionary? Russia has become a self-centered national state. The rank and file
of the people feel we wish the world revolution well, but would like to bring
order out of the chaos at home.

LECTURE 22
Social Composition of the Intellectuals,
Ideologies, Philosophy of the Populists

Last time I discussed the Russian intellectual. The Russian Revolution was the
handiwork of a small group of intellectuals who, because of a passive society,
were able to carry out their program.

SOCIAL COMPOSITION OF THE RUSSIAN INTELLECTUALS

A revolution in social composition: Russia acquired a class of people exposed
to Western ideas early in the nineteenth century. They were of the December
Revolution and were bringers of a new movement. The first intellectuals in
Russia came from the nobility, who had the means to educate their children.
The intellectuals from among the nobility developed a fine civilization. In
Russian literature there is reference to the social-minded intellectuals as repentant nobility. They repented the sins of their fathers. They were conscience-
striken. They repented the way their fathers exploited the peasants. The
repentant noblemen had a strong tendency to idealize the Russian peasant.
They thought of the peasant as Christians and living humans. Because they
idealized the peasants, these noble intellectuals were also prone to idealize the

commune. On the social side they thought Russia was advanced. In real socialization they felt the Russian peasants were not only equal to the West Europeans, but superior.

In the next generation—about the sixties and seventies—there arose a new type. They were no longer the repentant nobles, but were from the plebeian class. They were from all classes, sons of priests or petty officials, from among the lower classes or equal to the student who works his way through school. Being students and wearing student uniforms, they were treated like the rest and encouraged. These *plebeian intellectuals* held contempt for the earlier intellectuals, the noble intellectuals. The noble intellectuals did not know how to address the peasants. The peasants did not trust them. To the peasants the noble intellectuals were "funny birds." Thus, the noble intellectuals were looked down upon at every turn. They brought forth a coat of personality, individuality—a sort of ivory tower—an escapism. They developed a civilization hinging on personality.

The plebeian intellectuals did not like their predecessors and expressed their dislike by being rude—they kicked over the ivory tower. This was an effective group of people. The peasants did not trust them either. They had great energy and self-confidence and organized a revolutionary movement anyway, trusting that the peasants would catch fire. It resulted in the killing of the emperor. The combat was unique and unequal. Rule won. The movement was suppressed in the early eighties, and then there was a period of stagnation for ten years or so. In the nineties there awakened a spirit of independence. Rather a large group of university intellectuals comprised this group. Students were drawn into the movement in 1905. The labor revolutionary movement, the student intellectual movement, and the peasant movement—all were suppressed. However they revived in 1917. In the later period, many of the intellectuals were from among the peasants—teachers, doctors, and others.

There were two schools of ideologies: the People's school or the Populist (Russian word, *Narodnik*).[1] The other school was Marxism. The Narodnik school came first. Compare it to Marxism. Take for instance the interpretation of history. It was not a materialistic interpretation, but idealistic. It said history was moved by ideals and was conceived by great men who received these ideals. So instead of stressing mass movements, it stressed individuals—idealists. History was idealistic and the emphasis was on great personalities. There went with this idea social free will. Marx stressed the fact that the path was determined by the historical past and productive forces. In the populist view each nation has the power to choose the path it is to travel; it is not pushed by forces from behind. It can choose its own path—free will rather than determinism. It would choose its path through great leaders. Social free will had strong implication in Russia.

1. The People's party.

These intellectual socialists were opposed to capitalism. They skipped capitalism, saying the peasants have preserved the social order—the commune—but it is to be rounded out. They said Russia was lucky because it was not as advanced as France and other countries where the commune was gone and where society was torn by class struggles. Russia was spared all that because of its backwardness. "We have kept the village commune and we can use it as a foundation to erect socialism," they said. "We must not let capitalism enter Russia; we will skip capitalism, jump over it and go into modern socialism from the commune." How? Here the intellectuals had an important role. The idealist intellectuals constituted themselves as the guardians of Russia. They taught the peasants how to round out the commune, how to become cooperative producers, abandoning individual cultivation. Taught them to work cooperatively, pool labor, and a myriad of other things. Similarly regarding handicrafts. "We in Russia are blessed by the fact there are no urban industries. The peasants manufacture articles of consumption which the people need and so we teach them to cooperate. Neighbors get together or the whole village cooperates." Different cooperative groups were to specialize and freely exchange without need for the capitalist merchant. It would be voluntary socialism, a people's socialism, not a socialism of the state. A socialism of the people themselves; communes blossom out. The role of the state in the setup is there is no need for a central government. They were anarchists with the idea of no need for coercive government. Different groups would form larger and larger clusters as communes together—clusters woven around the social function or service to be rendered. The end would be the whole country as a freely federated entity. There would be a separate organ, not coercive in nature, to issue orders, taxes, and such. Control agencies would be just service institutions. Statistics would be collected as to how much was produced. Likewise a National Health Center, not armed with powers of a court-martial, but like a medical center in a social settlement in a modern country today. That is really your anarchistic type of society.

Why were so many outstanding anarchists from Russia? Some were Tolstoy and Kropotkin and Bakunin. All were from the nobility and from the agrarian society of Russia. All of them were deeply attached to the peasants. They were the repentant nobles and they idealized the peasants and knew of the commune. The village commune was the model or pattern before the eyes of the anarchists. In the village commune you could not see the government; it was an unorganized society. Order was kept spontaneously. There was an elder, but no one wanted the position. He was unpaid and had trouble if the village was in arrears in taxes. The soldier was in the commune and he flogged the peasants. The elder was flogged first. The commune was nongovernment. No one wanted to represent the government. Thus you can see why you would conclude no government in society. That was the kind of society the anar-

chists had in mind—a nongovernment society, but it was orderly. Also it was
a homogeneous society. Decisions had to be made, such as plowing of land,
but they were arrived at without political struggle. It was just management—
just common sense—harvest when harvest time was there, plow when the water
was off the land, and so forth. There did not have to be parliamentary law; all
talked at the meetings. It was a simple kind of administration, just plain common sense. That was the kind of society that the repentant nobles had had contact with and they had a tendency to idealize it. That was the type of society
the anarchists had in mind and the Populist party had this anarchist idea. They
did not want central government. The land went to the peasants, and they were
to administer it by communes and they were to be taught how to work together
and to live together. Another institution was the *artel.* This is an association of
peasants from the same village who would go to the big cities and take on a
labor contract. *Artel*: a labor cooperative that undertook a labor contract. They
share the proceeds and take them home. In the background was the neighborly
attitude from the village. The intellectual anarchists laid store by the *artel*—
social mindedness.

They had something in common with Marx, and a lot not in common. In
common were the social ideal and the classless society with no state. They did
not have in common the following: (1) to the Marxist a stage of proletariat
dictatorship (after a number of years the old ruling class would be gone, then
the proletariat dictatorship would be gone, then would come anarchism); (2)
to the Marxist, the proletariat was the revolutionary class. The Populists did
not have much use for the proletariat; they were interested in the peasants, in
the laboring intelligentsia as teachers, doctors, and such. They did not want
class division within the people. They had one common category—the people,
and they were the toilers. To them the basic category was the people. The
Marxist looked to the proletariat; he looked on other people as stupid and not
of revolutionary material.

The Populists and Marxists parted company. The Populists were anarchists
in philosophy; the Marxists were for anarchy for the future, but for the immediate, the proletariat dictatorship, and the proletariat was for revolution.

There was another basic point of difference—whether social-minded intellectuals should work for democracy, which included such things as civil liberties.
The Populists said no, we know what democracies are—a sham. In practice, it
is corruption of the government by the rich. So they said they did not want
democracy. "We have the village commune and let us broaden it out." Marxists
said this is all sentimentalist and non-realistic. They said the Populists think you
can skip the capitalistic stage, which is nonsense. The Marxists said that you
cannot skip capitalism. We must have democracy, too, in order to develop.

PART EIGHT
Groupings

LECTURE 23
The Marxists and the Populists

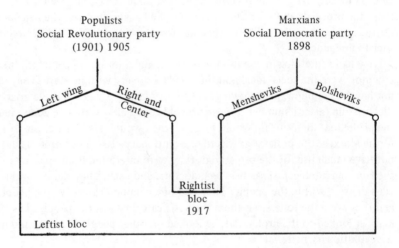

Populists
Social Revolutionary party
(1901) 1905

Marxians
Social Democratic party
1898

Left wing

Right and
Center

Mensheviks

Bolsheviks

Rightist
bloc
1917

Leftist bloc

YEARS OF REVOLUTION, 1905 AND 1917

The last time I discussed the philosophy of the Populists; they were anarchists—anarchists primarily because of their distrust of centralized government. They were the worshipers of the commune. The Marxists contradicted them all along the line. Populist philosophy existed in the sixties and seventies; Marxism came later. The first Marxist theorist was Plekhanov (1881). He started the school of Marxism in Russia. The Marxists said the Populists were sentimentalists, not realists. They said this because the Populists could not stand the idea of the hard school of factories, because of capitalism. They were too tender-minded to go through that, so they skip it and think that Russia can choose its own path. The Marxists said the Russian peasant must be cooked in the factory boiler, that before the peasant is fit material for socialism he must be proletarianized. They said the Russian peasant was not a real socialist. The Populist said the peasant was an embryonic socialist. By contrast the Marxist said the peasant is far from being an undeveloped socialist; he is an undeveloped individualist. They said the commune is far from being cherished and used, that the commune is a relic of barbarism. It had to be smashed in order to release the productive forces. So they said down with the commune—the peasant is an undeveloped individualist. It was the Marxist who brought out the fact that if Russian development is to be like France and the other countries, then next on the program was the bourgeois revolution. The next stage would be a bourgeois revolution; it would make a housecleaning of feudalism and absolutism and create a bourgeois democracy, and labor would be glad to see the bourgeoisie do that. The proletariat needs political freedom, the kind that exists under bourgeois democracy. The next thing would be the bourgeois revolution, which would dethrone feudalism and absolute government and give businessmen their heads to go ahead. Under a bourgeois system in Russia, the bourgeoisie would develop an industrial system. In order to do so the bourgeoisie must get rid of absolute government, and as a result the proletariat would benefit too. The proletariat would make good use of civil liberties and organize economically and politically, grooming itself for its own revolution. The proletariat would watch and bide its time and when its numbers increase enough and its organization was strong then it would claim its own candidate for the ruling class. All of this leads up to the proletariat revolution. The Marxists of that time thought the blueprint of Russia's future was the same as in other countries of the West—a capitalistic system and regime, and later on the proletariat revolution to liquidate capitalism, but there would be no jumps or bypassing the capitalistic stage. They must go through the capitalistic stage. It would be good training with peasants brought to the villages and cities and put through the industrial school. Then they would be good revolutionary material for modern socialist society.

Thus there were two different orientations and two different ways of thinking between the Populists and the Marxists. Also, two different emotional makeups. The Marxist was tough-minded; the Marxist was an intellectual snob. The Populist type was more hearty and humane—he did not stress correct dogma but sentiment. He was sympathetic. His sympathies wove around the human being. Marxist sympathies were around the abstract, the proletariat. Two human types, as well as divergent philosophies.

Marxism believed in mass movements and denied the creative role of the individual. A person was one of a class and rose and fell with the class. If the person were reactionary the system was to blame. If the reactionary were killed another would come forth, so that is not much good. Thus they did not believe in individual terrorism. They believed in mass movements (later, however, they resorted to mass terrorism).

The Populists believed that if there were a bad personality he should be gotten out of the way; if a cruel ruler, kill him. They practiced individual terrorism. This was no contradiction to sentiment. They killed high officials if they are guilty of great cruelty to the people. The Minister of the Interior was their target because he ordered peasant floggings. They went forth to kill the tyrant because of his cruelty to the people. So sentimentalism and terrorism went hand-in-hand. In killing they knew it was mortal sin, but they did it just the same.

The Marxists did not practice individual terrorism—not because they had kinder hearts but because the individual, they believed, did not make much difference. They believed in mass movements.

The Populists in the sixties and seventies thought at first that they could get what they wanted merely through peaceful persuasion. They did not kill at first; they were driven into it. They thought the peasants would take fire and respond to their ideals, and all would say what the people want and then the existing government would disappear. The voice of the people would cause the government to become ashamed and quit. This was a naive assumption; they soon realized it. The peasants did not react and often they tied up speakers to the peasants. The idealistic and peaceful revolutionaries discovered they could not ignore the existing government and they had to demand political freedom. They wanted to effect immediate transition from what existed to socialism. But they found the need for political freedom. In 1878 or 1879 they changed their philosophy. They changed from pure anarchism to political democracy. This was suppressed in the middle eighties but later rose again. They continued to march in two distinct schools of thought, two political organizations. A whole literature in Russian chronology is devoted to the debates of these two schools of thought. They would stage debates—however, debates in secret. The two groups continued separately.

DIVISION IN THE SOCIAL DEMOCRATIC PARTY

Just before he gave it, Marx's philosophy was opposed to the Populists; the Marxist called for a bourgeois revolution and then the proletariat revolution. By 1901 and 1902 there was a division in the Marxists themselves. The Bolsheviki (majority) were members of the majority. Mensheviki means minority. Both were small groups really. Also the margin which the majority had over the minority was a small one. In 1902 they held a conference in London and there split into two factions while retaining a common party designation. They split on what? They split on the qualifications for entering the revolutionary party (the Social Democratic party) and also the way in which the party was organized. Lenin's idea was that the party membership should be a select membership—professional revolutionaries—members who would devote their whole lives to the revolution, people with no other interest in life but just the cause. He wanted the revolutionary party to be like an army with iron discipline.

The Mensheviks were more liberal. They said anyone who was in sympathy with the party and had contributed to the party would be eligible. Then you would have a party of a large number of people whose chief life interest would be in making a living and who were devoted to the party, although the party would not be their all.

Management. Lenin believed in democratic centralism. An executive committee should have absolute power. Central leadership would be a permanent steering committee and it would control the party. Professionals could be run by super professionals, by iron discipline. Authority should descend from the top layer to the branches. The Mensheviks had the opposite idea—ascend. Lenin's idea was that the top authority would pressure the members.

It is the chancellor's business to get a majority in the Reichstag and he got it by pressure—got laws passed by pressure. This was Germany. Bismarck practiced democratic centralism. This was Lenin's idea. He argued that the party, after all, was illegal and operates under danger; the party thus runs as a dictatorship. Run the party as an army.

The Marxists were divided on the methods of inner party structure. To outsiders it looked like pedantry. This difference, however, was not just a mere detail—it was an important difference. What lay behind it was a basic difference in the outlook on life. The Mensheviks were basically afraid of anarchy. They felt revolution really meant anarchy, so they felt let's go slow. Do not unchain the beast (the people) because it might be destructive. They were forever favoring delay and intermediate stages. Thus they were pleading that the next revolution be a bourgeois revolution. Have an educated proletariat to lead into the proletariat revolution, and thus the danger to culture in general would be minimized. They did not say this, but it was what really operated. Lenin and his group were bolder. They were willing to take risks, they were not afraid of anarchy, they had confidence in themselves, they thought they could seize power. That was the psychological difference between the two groups.

One group was attached to Western culture and life, and they were afraid to open the floodgates in Russia on the uneducated people—everything would be swept away. The others were not afraid of that. That is what was really behind the difference. They had other arguments, but behind it all lay the psychological hinterland. The fear of anarchy of one group and the lack of fear on the part of the others. It was not a lack of courage, but one was fearful that the civilized way of life could be swept away and thus slow up the whole thing.

LECTURE 24
The Marxists and Division

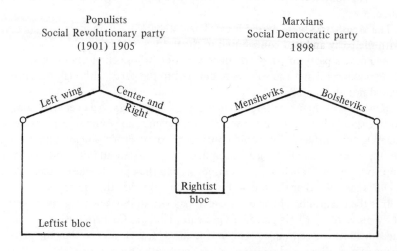

Marxists clashed horns with the Populists. The Marxists deride dependence on the peasantry. They said the commune was a relic of barbarism. They picture the Russian Revolution as a repetition of revolution in Western Europe. A bourgeois revolution and the establishment of a democratic regime based on capitalism. Then Russia would be industrialized on a large scale. Industrialization also means a rise of the proletariat, and the proletariat would take advantage of it to organize and get ready for the proletariat revolution. According to the Marxist, the Russian sequence is no different than that of Europe, only belated. He believed that the Russians had the advantage of Marxism; the process was clear and the strategy more to the point.

In 1902 or 1903 there was a division in the Marxist ranks—a division among those who had the will to revolution and the others who were held back by fear of premature action in Russia, the unpreparedness of the proletariat to play a big role. They kept putting it off. Lenin began to take part in the revolutionary movement in the early nineties. He was a strike leader in 1894 and 1895 and had indefatigable ability as a student and researcher. By 1901 or 1902 he conceived a different idea from the conventional Marxist idea. He was primarily impelled by burning revolution. His idea was that the next revolution in Russia would be a bourgeois revolution because it was a normal response. He said, take a look at the Russian bourgeoisie. They are bankers and factory owners and their like. They are to be the bridegroom of the next revolution. They do not look the part. They are scared to death because they see in Western Europe that the bourgeoisie is fighting with its back to the wall against the proletariat. In Western Europe the bourgeoisie would be glad now if it had by its side a strong feudal nobility which, in its thoughtlessness, it had destroyed. Lenin said the Russian bourgeoisie have no revolution in them. They are afraid. Thus the conventional bourgeois revolution is sure to sell out its own revolution. They will compromise with the landlord class and exact a few concessions for their own side. Essentially they are afraid to demand drastic changes in political organization as it is, and so realistically, one must discount them. So let us look at another class in Russia which we can use as a reliable substitute, and that is the peasantry—all peasants (rich, poor, and the middle class), peasantry as a whole, including the *kulaks* (rich upper strata). Peasantry as a whole hate the landlords because they have the land and there is no compromise between the peasantry and the landlords. (There cannot be a compromise.) The next revolution will be bourgeois, but the bourgeoisie is spiritless; here in Russia, substitute the peasantry and they can be relied upon. The peasantry is a revolutionary element. Lenin said the peasants are illiterate— so they need to have a guide and mentor, and that should be the proletariat. They (the proletariat) already have a revolutionary party and an intellectual possession. They have a Marxist interpretation and they grasp how society develops and their own role in it. So let the proletariat be the guardian. He advocates the *hegemony of the proletariat,* which means the guide, mentor, and leader.

That was Lenin's bourgeois revolution. A conventional bourgeois revolution would not work at all, but a bourgeois revolution in that the peasants participate. The proletariat will act as a political guide and mentor to the peasantry.

The regime that will emerge from this bourgeois revolution will be a *joint dictatorship of the proletariat and the peasantry.* The bourgeoisie is reactionary; so to give them political power would be silly. Do not toy with a democratic republic. Let us have joint dictatorship of the proletariat and the peasantry, and the proletariat will play the leading role. The peasantry will substitute for the conventional bourgeois revolution that had flunked out.

In the Marxist conception, after the bourgeois revolution there would be a period of economic development. For Lenin there was no need for such an interval. For Lenin there was no need for such an interval—the world productive forces had reached the form which the bourgeoisie form restricted—the world was getting internally ready for the proletariat revolution. Look at the world as a unit being ready, then Russia is isolated. Since that is the case, the Russian bourgeois revolution with the proletariat as its head would hasten world-wide revolution. He said that the day after the bourgeois revolution we would begin the world proletariat revolution. Revolution means the driving of a wedge between the rich and the poor peasants, and the proletariat could do it. The proletariat would ally themselves with the poorer peasants and would be against the rich peasants, and that would be the proletariat revolution in Russia. In Western Europe the proletariat would rise against the bourgeoisie and put over revolution. This is the Leninist conception. It modifies Marx's theory in order to justify immediate revolution without the conventional bourgeoisie in the picture, with an immediate proletariat revolution. The will to revolution guided his thinking.

The Mensheviks said Lenin was betraying the Marxists. They said what matters is to live up to the substance of theory. Russia needed the contribution of the untrampled bourgeoisie in order to develop productive forces. They said Lenin was dealing with theoretical trickery. The two groups parted company intellectually and, really, temperamentally. In 1903 when the separation took place there were two factions. Earlier they had warred over the constitution of the party, for example, who would be eligible to join the party. Lenin had held out for iron discipline whereas the Mensheviki would admit anybody. Lenin insisted on authority at the top and the Mensheviks were willing to have the authority come from below. At the time it looked to the people like quibbling over details, but it was anything but that. If you accept Lenin's revolution without an interval and compromise and the proletariat exercising hegemony (the Social Democrat party), this meant the need for a party of iron discipline with professional revolutionaries. Lenin had a vigorous conception of revolution. The Mensheviki idea of the party was that it was composed of a lot of people not professionally revolutionary and with the concept of an interval of social peace between the capitalistic revolution and the proletariat revolution. They had a milder concept with milder discipline. Also they held the concept of nonprofessional revolutionists and authority from below which was in harmony with the Mensheviki. To outsiders the struggle looked like madness. I was reading magazines at the time and when I read them I felt like it was a reading of theology, a quarreling over something not very important. The reading was salty but it looked like over-salting. At that time it seemed to me that way, but now I see it was different.

The revolutionary ranks were divided into two factions; each faction really was a small group of intellectuals. The Russian social body had no resistance; thus when the factions started swinging into action they were able to win.

The Populists had an anarchistic conception and found a need for political freedom and they began to demand political democracy (the right wing). It was a democratic republic they wanted with the peasantry dominating. You must turn the private estates into communes. They would see to it that the peasantry was not converted into a landless proletariat. They would keep the peasants united. Capitalism in the cities did not appeal to them, but it was there so they accepted it. Keep it, but keep urban capitalism in the cities and not allow it to penetrate into the country. The factory workers were peasants too, so they said they were okay. The majority were tied or kept ties to their villages. They wanted the overthrow of the aristocracy and a peasant government. A peasant government would see to it that the commune flourished and urban capitalism would not become too strong, and by and by it would be replaced with a cooperative system. Now they talked in terms of a democratic form of political organization. Earlier they had said communes and voluntary alliances would exist and at the center a series of service bureaus. This was the anarchist conception. Now they swing away from that and toward democracy. By *1904 and 1905* a split in the group resulted. There was the left, which was a throwback to the earlier anarchism. They said that under the new formulation you might survive under a democracy dominated by the peasant and keep capitalism out and by and by develop—that is meaningless. It will not work. We must go back and not entrust ourselves to democracy. At that time the French syndicalists were going strong. Anarchist political theory was in the ascendancy in certain circles. The left wingers said we will go back to the anarchist conception; we want socialism right now. This division took place in the Social Revolutionary party.

The year 1917. There was a revolutionary move in 1905 and it had failed. In 1917 the aristocracy fell because it was incapable of coping with the war problem. The Liberals appointed a Provisional government—a shadow. The real government was the Soviet with its officials and the council. Struggle resulted in the Soviet. Party struggle resulted in the Soviet with its assembly of delegates selected by factory workers and regiments. In the Soviet every party was represented. The majority was in the hands of the Rightist bloc,[1] those who had a milder conception of revolution. They got together on the idea that Russia should be an advanced democracy. There would be no disfranchised class; all would have the same political rights. In the economic order of Russia, do not rush things. It was a foregone conclusion that land would be given to the peasants, but it was not right to take the factories from the owners and give them to the workers, because that would be to jump the gun. They also agreed on one issue as being important—war and peace. The country had been at war two and one-half years, and they had sacrificed themselves for the preservation of culture in Europe. They had repeated their performance in the thirteenth century when they had cushioned Europe from the Mongol invasion. In the twelfth and thirteenth centuries Russia had first played its role as shield to Western Europe; the second time in 1914 under World War terms; and now again Russia was doing the job for Western civilization. The Russian people were wearied from the First World War. The Rightist bloc did not quite understand the longing of the people for peace. They, too, wanted to end war but they did not want to leave the Allies, so they urged the Allies to make peace but they were still staying in the war.

The Leftist bloc,[2] led by the Bolsheviks, showed itself much more attuned to persuasion of mass psychology. They knew the three wishes of the people:

1. In the diagram at the beginning of the chapter, it will be recalled, the Rightist bloc consisted of both the Mensheviks and the Center and Right of the Social Revolutionary party.
2. As noted earlier in the diagram, the Leftist bloc was composed of both the Bolsheviks and the Left wing of the Social Revolutionary party.

(1) immediate peace, (2) the peasants' desire for land, and (3) the factory workers', wage earners', desire to get even—to lay hands on employers economically. The bloc worked for that. They went along with the psychological current. The Bolsheviks made an alliance with the Left wing of the Social Revolutionary party. Their outlooks were not the same. but they both shared the desire to end war and make a clean sweep of the existing institutions, including the bourgeois order of things. By October 1917 Trotsky was elected President of the Petrograd Soviet, which meant a Leftist majority (Lenin's side in control). Trotsky was not a Bolshevik until the summer of 1917. He held a line of reasoning like Lenin's, and discounted the bourgeois revolution. He said it was up to the proletariat to put over the bourgeois revolution; but when the proletariat got the swing of things it would not stop with liquidating in Russia but would go on to world revolution. The only difference between Lenin's and Trotsky's views of revolution was that Trotsky had no place for the peasantry. He would do it all with the proletariat; aside from that Trotsky and Lenin were the same. Trotsky disdained the peasants; he would use the proletariat. They had the same timetable otherwise and the will to revolution. Lenin's blueprint of revolution came to pass in 1917-18 and 1920—not because Lenin was such a good astronomer, but because he knew how to pull the ropes.

LECTURE 25
The Rightist and Leftist Struggle

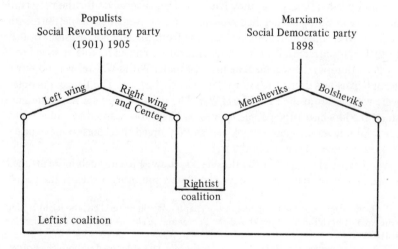

There was a struggle in the summer of 1917 between the Rightist and the Leftist. The Rightist stood for a democratic Russia. It solved the land problem in favor of the peasants and offered Russian labor a favorable springboard for future revolution. The Rightist coalition conception was that Russia was not yet ready for the liquidation of capitalism. The Leftist conception was that Russia was quite ready to liquidate capitalism. Lenin said we are going through with the bourgeois revolution. He was quite determined that on the day following the bourgeois revolution the world proletariat revolution would begin.

There were two programs, one more moderate and one more radical. We usually say in the West that moderates are more realistic than radicals; usually this is the rule. Moderates take into account the existing institutions. So in Western Europe and America the moderate version of the socialistic program was more realistic, but in Russia the more realistic was the radical. This was because friction did not have to be taken into account; there was a lack of resistance. The radical program in Russia was more realistic than the moderate. All the more realistic since tossing out the bourgeois revolution, the radical group was able to cater to the wishes of the masses at the time. Some examples were the craving for peace and the peasants' hunger for land and the factory workers' desire for revenge against the exploiters. (1) An absence of friction or resistance was the product of Russia's history. (2) The leaders of the Rightists tried to hold in check the pent-up emotions of the people. The Rightists said stay in the war and hasten peace, but Lenin was more realistic. He knew how much the people wanted peace. Lenin saw that the people wanted peace. The radical group was with the grain of the masses rather than against the grain. The radicals won out—not only in the Petrograd Soviet but later in the test of civil war. They said, we can toss the bourgeois out of the picture. They seized power in October 1917. The two allies were the Bolsheviks and the Left wing of the Social Revolutionary party. The Left wing was a throwback to the anarchism of the seventies. The Bolsheviks, for reasons of opportunism took the Leftist agrarian program of the other party and made it theirs in the interest of alliance with the Left wing. The Left wing wrote an agrarian edict. It reproduced the old Populist conception of the commune. All estates were turned over to the village communes, thrown into the jackpot, and communes applied the same system of allotment as had been done before. The old dream of Populism, to see the landlord uprooted, for once came true. Ninety-nine percent of the land in Russia, after the edict, came under the control of the village commune.

The two groups ruled jointly. While the immediate program was the same due to compromise, basically the outlook was divergent. The Bolshevik world revolution outlook was an international outlook. Their allies had a national outlook, concerned with the problems of Russia. They wanted to disentangle

Russia from the rest of Europe. They were isolationists—let's build Russia as a
model for the rest of the world. The Bolsheviks said Russia was a part of the
world arena and it was possible to puncture Russian capitalism—let us use
Russia for a world-wide revolution. They differed on the question of government. The Social Revolutionary group wanted a maximum of self-government—
clusters of voluntarily affiliated groups and the whole country a free federation
of self-governing groups, but without bureaucracy. The center agencies would
serve as service agencies. The chief interest would be the peasants.

The two parties broke within a year and broke on the question over resistance to the Germans. Lenin thought that when the Russian proletariat seized
power, the proletariat would do likewise in Germany and Austria; but they
did not. Thus Lenin had to deal with the militarists of Germany. He had to let
Germany take the Ukraine. Lenin accepted Brest-Litovsk because he wanted a
breathing spell. He was willing to surrender thirty million peasants to Germany.
The parties broke on that, and in July 1918, congress convened and these parties broke apart.

I got an account of the debate from a person I spoke with. There was a break
in the parties. The Left wing of the Social Revolutionary party was indignant.
They indicted Lenin and others for their heartlessness in surrendering the peasants. They charged that the peasants were used as mere pawns. By the second
day they were ready to revolt against the government with which they were
allied. The secret service of the Bolshevik party was quite good; they arrested
the leaders and the fighting organization of the Left wing of the Social Revolutionary party. There was a break between the two parties.

There are several phases of subsequent revolution. The phase of the revolution between 1918 and 1922—the Bolsheviks called this phase the War of
Communism. The new regime was obliged to fight two kinds of war; one was
foreign intervention. There were foreign armies in Russia. Also there were
counter-revolutionary armies—the White armies. The last one was destroyed
in 1920. Foreign wars were by the intervention of former allies of Russia,
and civil war; and the Polish won (took the city of Kiev).

The Bolsheviks, who later called themselves Communists, refer to the war
as the War of Communism. Their economics were mere emergencies. They had
nationalized all the factories in Russia and had theoretically nationalized the
land (the communes had land). That led to complete disorganization in Russian industry and a drop in productivity. By 1921 the production dropped 17
percent from the 1913 basis. Russia could stand this because a small percent of
the people were urban. Also, the factory workers had their own place they
could go to—to the villages. That is why the people could stand the Russian
contraction of productivity. The village was a meal ticket, and it was that that
saved the country. During those years the big industries were conducted as
state enterprises, partners of the government. Wages were paid in provisions

and not in money. Money was losing its value. The government was aiming at
an economy where the labor of each citizen would be at the disposal of the
government and, likewise, the government would assume the position of
feeding and provisioning; eventually this would be without the interference of
money. A portion of the city people went to the villages. Still some remained
in the cities, such as the officials, who had to be fed. There was, then, a levy on
the peasants. The government sent out armed guards to the village districts to
make requisitions. The peasants paid in paper money which was not worth
much. The government had to do this to feed armies and take care of its other
problems. Thus, gradually the peasant lost his gratitude to the government.
The government gave him land, but now the government was sending men—
armed men—to take his foodstuffs. The peasant turned against the government.
The government at first was nice but now it had changed. The peasant seized
upon a plausible explanation—the Bolshevik party. In the middle of 1919 the
Bolsheviks changed their name to Communists. Marx called himself a Communist to distinguish himself from the wishy-washy socialists. Similarly Lenin's
party in 1919 felt it should differentiate itself from the wishy-washy Social
Democrats and changed its name to Communists. The peasants jumped to the
conclusion that a change had taken place. The Bolsheviks had been okay, after
all they had given out the land. But they were against the Communists because they took away food and their means of subsistence. The peasants were
for the Bolsheviks but against the Communists. The peasant was in a dilemma.
Should he side with the counter-revolutionaries? They would take his land.
Finally he decided to support the new government because he wanted land
and it was more important than food. The siding of the peasants with the new
government was basically important in determining the outcome of the war.
The peasant decided to side with the new government. He began to fear requisitions and the like. Once the fear of the landlord's returning was dispelled, his
grievances against the new government grew stronger. In the 1920s the peasants
were rebellious against the requisitions; and the sailors, being peasants themselves, rebelled against the new government and demanded free Soviets—free
elections. The Soviet system was based upon popular representation. It worked
in such a way that it was controlled. The sailors demanded that the will of the
people be heeded and that the elections be free. Trotsky was Minister of War.
He was the organizer of the Red army and was largely responsible for the defeat of the White army. Trotsky at that time was second to Lenin in power,
and he was not a gentle person. He sent an army to defeat the sailors and it
was a bloody scene. The sailors were defeated.

Lenin learned an important lesson from the peasant rebellions and from the
Kronstadt sailors. The experiment with Communism was premature. It had to
make a retreat. To treat property as national property was the undoing of Russia. While the party was in power, there was the NEP to appease the peasants.

The peasants had the right to lead their own lives, use land acquired according to their customs, and to pay a fixed tax to the government in goods. It was limited to 10 percent of the crops, and the balance they could dispose of as they saw fit. The peasants were allowed to consume and sell crops. Up to that time—1918 to 1921—no transactions in the market were permitted. Now, with the new economic policy, they could trade. This really was a retreat of the party.

Period of NEP. This was an economic appeasement primarily directed at the peasants. There were other features too: permission for smaller shops to be operated by their owners; factories grouped as trusts and operated on a balance sheet with credit from the government bank, but they had to pay for the credit. There were trading operations. Currency was used. The ruble was made firm. Communist Russia now blossomed forth with good currency.

Commentators of the world scene said that Russia now had learned a lesson—it could not do without capitalism, and capitalism was to be re-erected. This was not so. Lenin made a concession to the peasants. His idea was that once agriculture and industry were back to normal, then a new day would dawn. Lenin's idea of the NEP was that it would prove merely a temporary retreat and would be followed later by a bolder policy.

Lenin died in 1924 and the NEP continued. Power fell into the hands of Stalin. The NEP continued from 1924 to 1929. There had been three basic tendencies in the Communist party within three years.

PART NINE
The Communist Party

LECTURE 26
The NEP, the Death of Lenin,
and Struggles within the Party

Last time we covered an account of the Russian Revolution down to the economic policy, the NEP. The first phase was civil war and an attempt to introduce Communism in quick order by abolishing the category of quick (individual) income. As far as the peasant was concerned, he worked for himself but could not consider his crops as his own. He was subject to levy by the government for the needs of the government in supplying the army and urban population. The coming of the NEP changed that; it was a retreat on the economic front. The peasant was permitted an individual economy. He could trade or sell his crops. Likewise a re-entry into individual enterprise in the smaller productive units was allowed. NEP was a concession to the peasants. It was not as foreigners thought, that Russia had found a need for capitalism. As a matter of fact, big industries were not returned to their owners but were operated as public corporations. Trusts and management were appointed by the government and had to make ends meet, entailing the holding down of costs. The workers were paid in money. Basically the essence of the new economic policy was to permit the peasant to practice a degree of individualism that he was accustomed to (he could now own land) and the Communist party could continue its role as a political party. How long the plan would last was not known. Many leading Bolsheviks thought it would last a long time.

The new economic policy sided with the quieting of the world revolutionary front. In 1920 world revolution reached its peak. The near capture of Warsaw was one of the high marks and another was the occupation of the factories by workers in northern Italy. Those were the two highest formations of revolutionary possibility outside of Russia. By 1921 the high water wave was receding. In 1921 things were quieting down on the revolutionary front. In the ensuing two or three years there were developments from time to time which did keep the hope for revolution alive. Germany was an example, with its struggle. Subsequent developments after 1921 tended to keep the hope for world revolution up. But after 1920 it was evident, for the time being at least, world revolution was quieting down. The Hungarian Soviet was put down.

The center of attention, naturally, was on Russia itself. Agriculture was quickly reviving; industry not so quickly. In agriculture, 1922–23, the volume of output of 1913 was reached. Industry waited until 1925–26 before the level of output of 1913 was reached. Urban populations, such as that of Leningrad, which had left the city and gone to the villages, came back to the cities and found work.

Lenin died in January 1924. He really held the party together by his moral and intellectual prestige. They all knew he had great practical sense. They knew if he said retreat it was not because he was afraid, but because of his analysis of the forces at the time. While Lenin lived other parties were gradually eliminated. In the Communist party itself there was freedom of expression and thought. Lenin did use strong discipline. Once a decision was made he expected cessation of debate. Under Lenin party life was dynamic and virtually free, except that an issue once decided was not to be brought up again.

When he died many people thought the Russian regime would fall. They did not know Russian history. When he died rivalry between factions in the party came about because people were no longer moderated by his influence. Personal issues came to the front, such as that between Stalin and Trotsky. It was a time when the fight between personalities began. But in view of the old climate of Marxism, all such rivalries had to be expressed as struggles over party policy. It was a long time before it became proper for members of the party to indulge in the adulation of individuals. Lenin was adverse to it. The respect his associates felt for him was expressed by agreeing with him after they heard his views in opposition to theirs; they then accepted his opinion.

At Lenin's death the moral climate of the party underwent a change. There was a dangerous, somewhat vulgar strain within the party—not just rivalries between persons but clashes of outlooks and orientations. The most outstanding was that of Stalin and Trotsky. There was an antithesis. By outlook Trotsky was a western European intellectual. He spent many years in western Europe. He spoke many languages. He was familiar with Western culture. To him the center of gravity of our society was western Europe. For him to think of a Communist revolution confined to backward Russia, with western Europe not in it, was just a monstrosity—a monstrous thought. If Russia alone built a new society and not western Europe, then the whole thing was a mockery. To him socialism was to be the acme of modern culture. To western European intellectual life, the world revolution was the paramount concern. He understood why the Russian capitalistic system was the first to be broken, but for him to think the proletariat revolution could start in Russia and be confined there for a time was unbearable.

Stalin was self-educated and could write. He lacked the brilliance of Trotsky. Stalin had a brief sojourn in western Europe for a few weeks. He came from a backward part of Russia and did not feel that western Europe was the center of the world. To him the thought of a socialist system for an indefinite period built up and confined to Russia was not an unbearable thought. For Stalin it was quite possible to come forth with socialism in one country. For Trotsky socialism in one country was psychologically impossible because of his orientation.

Other leading figures changed sides. Some were with Stalin. There were the three horses, Stalin, Kamenev, and Zinoviev. Trotsky was brilliant and could sway crowds and individuals and on that he depended. In the years 1923-25, crucial years when there was a struggle to lead, Trotsky depended upon his personal prestige. Stalin was a somber person with no ability to attract hero worship, but he was a great organization man and built up a personal machine by shoving around the secretariats.

STRUGGLES WITHIN THE PARTY ON THE SIDE OF IDEALS

There are three lines of interpretation as to what was happening in Russia at the time. Each group, before proposing an injunction of policy, was obliged to state its own appraisal of the trends of the revolution.

The Left wing or Trotsky appraisal viewed the revolution as fraught with great danger to Russia itself. It was present in 1925-26. To Trotsky the revolution was in danger because the bourgeois elements were growing in size and weight, which would eventually liquidate the revolutionary elements or the NEP elements, especially the peasants—the richer ones, the kulaks. The kulaks were the future liquidators of the Russian Revolution. For the time being they were lying low and making money and not making any political demands. But Trotsky said they were biding their time and we Communists are permitting them to grow strong. According to him, the Soviet Revolution should widen its own base by industrialization. He said the only political class reliable was the proletariat, the factory workers. Strengthen the proletariat and siphon away from the richer peasantry the capital they are accumulating. Put capital into nationally conducted large industries. This will serve two purposes: (1) industrialize Russia and (2) enlarge the numbers of factory workers who are the best support of the Soviet regime. He advocated speedy industrialization and the taking of capital from the peasants. How to do it? By the price system. Under NEP what the peasant sold were at prices set by the government. If a government put prices low, it would thus siphon. Simultaneously, industrialization would enlarge the proletariat and make the higher peasants harmless. The government should expedite collectivism—agriculture from individual enterprise to collective enterprise—and that would be done at the same time as mechanization. The government would make tractors and such and build up a mechanical agriculture.

The Trotsky program included on the agricultural front, the absorption of the peasant savings and the collectivism and mechanization of agriculture. It sought to widen industry and the proletariat. When Trotsky surveyed the developments in Russia, he viewed the whole theory with alarm.

The Rightist faction pointed with pride to the achievements of the Revolution. It countered Trotsky by saying we do not need to be afraid of the kulaks. We are using them; by giving them free enterprise we are getting a surplus for Russia. Give the kulak just enough economic freedom so that he has an incentive to produce a surplus, forever keeping him under our thumb because we control the trade. Keep a thumb on the peasant's windpipe. Furthermore, why be nervous? We are quite safe because the Soviet state holds the commanding heights. We have government operation of foreign and wholesale trade, and systems of communication and transportation, and big industry, and we control the prices. Set prices on what the peasants sell and prices on the manufactured articles the peasants must buy. Thus we are safe from what Trotsky says is dangerous. The Rightist idea of future development of socialism says it will come gradually. The peasant would be brought over by playing upon his own interests. Get collectivism by enticing him with mechanization; give him a tractor et cetera. It would be painless growing into socialism as far as the peasants are concerned. This view was the view of the Right. That was the intellectual struggle in the 1870s.

Stalin was in between, building up his organization and playing on personal jealousies, such as that between Trotsky and others. Stalin was in the party before Trotsky and he played on that. Stalin got rid of Trotsky by combining with the Right wing and in 1927 Trotsky was expelled from the party and exiled.

The victory over Trotsky was accompanied by the adoption of his program by Stalin. Stalin did it with a vengeance, so much so that the program was carried out with force. It was the first *Five Year Plan*. In building a big dam and obtaining electricity, it made a beginning. In 1929 Stalin's first Five Year Plan was followed by a second Five Year Plan. It forced a draft into industrialization and it was responsible for Russia's now being able to withstand Germany. Hence industrialization and collectivism was a Five Year Plan.

LECTURE 27
Stalin's Program

Last time I discussed the great struggle in the Communist party. Trotsky was brilliant and oriented toward the West. Stalin was an organizational man—a party boss—shrewd and realistic. Socialism for one country versus world revolution on the front. Stalin was right in his policy. Trotsky's policy would only have led to catastrophe. Stalin turned away from world revolution, not giving it up, just turning to a more practical line. In doing so he adopted with vigor and exaggeration the economic part of the Trotsky program with regard to class policy in Russia. This was, namely, industrialization and the collectivism of agriculture. He adopted the collectivism of agriculture on such an enormous scale and fast tempo that Trotsky himself was aghast. Trotsky wanted to kill the kulak danger, or individualism, and do it by shaking down the kulak with a price system and collective agriculture. Do it if you collectivize and you could then proceed with mechanization; but he never intended for the agriculture collectives to ride on the peasant's half-starved horse. Trotsky said Stalin's adoption of speedy collectivization showed that bureaucracy and the proletariat were capable.

It was an economic program that was costly in human lives and welfare. The population was on a diet of consumer goods. What England had gone through, now the Russians were subjected to in 1929. Factors of production, labor, capital, and goods, were diverted from consumer industries to producer industries, especially to the construction of plants. The impact of modern war in totally reshaping the economy, as far as Russia was concerned, began in 1929. Was it as Trotsky said at the time—just a bureaucratic ruthlessness with no regard for the human—or a far-sightedness to prepare Russia for future attack? Admirers of Stalin say it is far-sightedness—the first Five Year Plan and the second Five Year Plan.

I have a negative judgment. That is not the dominant motive; in 1927, 1928, and 1929, when plans were considered and adopted, in those years when Russians spoke of foreign intervention, whom did they have in mind? The enemy was England and France. There were placards reading, "Down With Chamberlain." Realistically speaking, one could not work oneself into a state of nerves over Austen Chamberlain and France. It was not just farsightedness, because the war Russia is fighting now is a total war—the nation is on dry beans. In the years 1928 and 1929 no one dreamed of such total war. German officers and Russian officers talked of a new type of war. I doubt if even the German officers had a conception of total war. I think the first Five Year Plan and the second Five Year Plan were not militarily inspired. There were some military features. The military danger, however, was not on the scene to cause disaster and a change in the use of resources. The program was inspired by the thoroughness of a person who knows he can go as far as he likes without opposition. That was exactly possible for Peter the Great two hundred years earlier. It was the *pattern of Peter the Great* with his forcible Westernization rather than foreseeing the might of Hitler.

The thing was put over, and put over largely because of the nonexistence of real centers of resistance. In some regions the peasants tried passive resistance by not plowing fields. The government did collect the usual quota from the peasants, regardless of the shortage of crops. For the peasants it was famine. As a punitive measure, the kulaks were sent north to build roads. The thing was put over at a great cost and can be called a practical program. If it had failed, maybe there would have been a different judgment.

Stalin built a new civilization in Russia, and we now see how he managed to forge a new nation with love for the land they live in. No one has the right to say that it was just barbarism; barbarism did accompany it from western European and American ethics, but it was constructive. It served as construction for a new civilization. In many regards this new Stalin Russia reminds one of the United States after the Civil War and during the period of Grant. The periods have in common a tremendous economic expansion. It was a technological industrial revolution. In the United States it took place by private ownership, in Russia by national ownership. In the United States it was planless; in Russia it was planned by the government.

I am using the term Industrial Revolution in a certain sense as did Napoleon I. To him the Industrial Revolution was the subordination of agriculture to industry. He did not stress the rise of the capitalists. He stressed, in his concept, the technological and social aspects. Industry first and agriculture second in national wealth and income and social progress. Russia and the United States had in common a subordination of agriculture to industry. In the United States many of the industrialists were business buccaneers and in Russia they were politicians assisted by technicians and engineers. Foreigners were hired for their skills. The revolution in the United States was put over by the politically powerful and ruthless businessmen. In Russia the revolution was through political leaders with the aid of technical talents and abilities. They hired abroad or raised the talent in their own institutions. A Russian dam that was famous (and blown up a year ago) was built by an American engineer.

They had another thing in common: the attitude of individuals. Individualism was rampant. The individual felt it his privilege to look after his own career. He becomes rich and powerful. He feels no ethical obligation to hold himself in check for the sake of others. Restriction upon well seeking that guilds enforced or trade unions enforced was absent in expanding capitalist industrialism in America. That made for a "pushy" individual, and a go-getter type developed. There was no social reason to hold him back; he could go ahead by hook or crook to build up the country. Thus there was an ethical justification. And there existed a sense or system of values—ruthless individualism, but there was the feeling that it was good for the country (as in the case of Rockefeller or Carnegie).

People tell me the new type of Russian is ruthless and energetic. The old type was slothful, inactive. The passivity is gone. It is all drive now. You think you are in a boomtown in the United States. All *drive now.* Drive for a career. The young people are not ashamed about getting on. In my days it was vulgar to talk about a career and its advantages. Now the individual is not ashamed of planning a career and rising to the top as fast as he can. In the United States during the post-Civil War period there was a foreshadowing of the Russia under Stalin. There is a psychology of expansion and no feeling that the individual should be rationed as regards the amount of opportunity. (There is an anti-individual group ethic if opportunity is scarce. If there is a lot of opportunity the person gets ahead.) There is unashamed individualism and careerism. The United States' post-Civil War period and Stalin's Communism have something in common. The United States after the Civil War—the country—was built up fast. Within the legal framework of a publicly owned economy in Russia you have the same thing; strong men forced their ways to the top.

I do not sympathize with that kind of an attitude. In prerevolutionary time in Russia there was an intellectual sensitiveness. I will not go back to Russia because I do not want to see the coarsening effect. I have respect for Stalinistic Russia for its strength, but it is a different civilization. It is stronger than the intellectual civilization of prerevolutionary Russia. That was bankrupt and showed it in August of 1917. The period from May 1917 to October 1917 expressed itself in Kerensky. He represented the intellectual civilization; he was reluctant to employ force. The Russian revolution was to be peaceful; he hoped for a new order without bloodshed—by common consent of idealistic people. That failed; it could not come to be. Instead there was the triumph of Trotsky and Lenin. A tug-of-war had occurred between the tougher and the tenderer minded.

It is a different civilization, a stronger civilization. Leaders have arisen from the ranks of workers and peasants. They are not bothered by doubts. They have the courage of ignorance. A simplified stereotype of the outside world. All of those who do not belong to the Communist party are hirelings of the capitalists. I wonder if they were surprised at the action of England in June of 1941 when Churchill sided with Russia. Also, Churchill has just said use gas against Germany if Germany uses it against Russia.

The order Stalin has built is a tough order. It has realized in its own way the bringing of the strong to the top from all elements, especially from the working class.

Is western Europe going to go Communist? Many people talk that way now. The only country that is effective in fighting against the Fascists is Russia. Russia controls Germany by prestige and armies, and so many people feel Europe will go Communist. Thus many people hesitate in giving aid to Russia. They would rather see the war end in a draw so they will see their own way of life saved.

My idea is that there really is no danger or probability of western Eurepean countries going Communist. Why? First, take the oppressed occupied countries like France and Norway. The most burning emotion there is the emotion to regain national freedom. They are oppressed not as workers or proletariat but oppressed as nationals, so when the Nazi nightmare breaks apart, their foremost wish is to have free expression of their nation. The first outburst after the downfall of Hitler will be nationalism. Nationalism is an opponent of Communism. The suppression of nations will result first in an upsurge of nationalism rather than Communism.

Another reason there is no probability of the Russian system extending is that each government must discharge as basic to its people the provisioning of food. When the war ends and Germany collapses, who will have the breadbasket of Europe? Not Russia, because she herself is on the ragged edge. The Ukraine is the breadbasket of Russia, and it is occupied. It is a puzzle to me how Russia is feeding her people now. When the war ends Russia will be victorious militarily but it will be a hungry victor.

The United States and Canada have food, food as a weapon. With food as a weapon one is able to control the political life of emancipated countries. There is a danger of resurrection of extreme nationalism. The United States, with food as a weapon, will have to use it to force the European nations to moderate nationalism, to forego Communism.

This analysis is more pro-Russia in substance; to predispose us to give aid to Russia. More so than those who are for the Russian system and extol it, and then paralyze aid to Russia. Our people do not want to assist Russia to the borders of the European continent.

In the next period I will give attention to the economics of Marx.

PART TEN
Value

LECTURE 28
The Marxian Theory of Economic Equilibrium

SUMMARY OF MARXIAN ECONOMICS

I have stressed history, politics, and imperialism in the course of the semester. Now I intend to examine economics—the Marxian theory of equilibrium. *Theory*: Economic equilibrium is the theory of value and price. Wages and profit and rent. The Marxist theory of economic equilibrium. The second part is the theory of capitalist dynamics. Under the first consideration we will try to take a snapshot of the capitalist system as Marx tries to give it. The second is a moving picture and study of its dynamics, especially with reference to the changing structure.

Marx wished to achieve a social science; other economists did also. They wanted to achieve an economic science. He was in the classical tradition in trying to erect an economic science of life. Science—what kind served as a yardstick? What was the science—astronomy and physics—a physical science, a science of matter and motion? A special slant of human volition or even divine volition was out of the picture. No one higher up was pulling strings. The cosmos was automatic. There is automatic balance. Cosmic bodies themselves produce cosmic order. In approaching a social problem or a problem of a science of society—from the standpoint of the eighteenth century—you rule out caprice; you want an objective science. A science dealing with phenomena without caprice. Subjective valuations (the theory we were brought up on) of buyers and sellers arrive at value by the intersection of two curves. To Marx this was ridiculous because of caprice. A Marxist says, yes, you might arrive at price that way but you do not arrive at the real fundamental basic value. Classical economists and Marx, in studying value, would not pay much attention to the subjective valuations. Marx says that we study the level of the ocean and take into account oscillations. A Marxist, in order to formulate a

113

theory of value, wants to get away from subjective valuations and looks to something independent of human volition or caprice. He sees a world of commodities and tries to find out what determines the ratio of exchange of one commodity to the other. Here one commodity appeals to its consumers but that falls into the category of whimsy. Find out a common yardstick to determine the ratio of one to the other of the commodities. Labor? Then what kind of labor? Clothes exchanged for cabinets—two labors? How can you measure the difference? Reduce them to a common basis. Reduce labor to a common denominator and you have what Marx calls abstract labor—the outflow of human energy productively employed. The outpouring of labor's energy is abstracted from a particular kind of labor or skills. Abstract labor is an outflow of purposely directed human energy.

Take into account that the methods of production do not stand still; they change. The Industrial Revolution expedited the productive process. If you say abstract labor and the value of commodity *A* as to *B* is determined by the quantity of labor each contains, then the greater labor the greater the value. But that is not enough. Suppose you have in the same market two products—one is by hand and one is by machine. If you look at the handicraft, say a desk, the time it took if by hand is a large lump, but if by machine, a smaller lump because it takes less time to produce the desk. Which lump shall we take to measure? The large lump or the small? Marx says you take whatever is the dominant mode of production. As in China today, you would take handicraft, or the larger lump. In the United States where machine production is dominant, you would take the smaller lump. Marx's value is determined not only by the quantity of the frozen lump of abstract labor but also the mode of production. Marx says in capitalistic society the social necessity takes care of the mode or matter of production. The social necessity determines the length of time.

Another thing is the varying degree of efficiency of the workman and of the shops. It is the average, the average length of time. The value of the article is determined by the average length of time it takes to produce under the dominant mode of production. Marx says commodities exchange on value. Later he talks of exploitation. In the process of exchange he looks away from exploitation. He assumes in exchange the commodities exchange on true value.

Specific commodity. Labor power is the commodity the wage earner sells to the employer. What is the value of 'labor power? The value of other commodities is measured by the lump of frozen labor—the mode and efficiency. Labor power? Marx makes a distinction between labor and labor power. Labor is the process, the flow of labor energy. Labor power is inseparable from the individual who works. Labor creates value. Labor is value itself. Labor power has value, it has commodity. Labor is a process, flow of energy, but labor power has value as commodity. The value of labor power is the sum total of value of commodities and services to create it. The value of labor power is the sum total of food, clothing, and such—the total value of the commodities that go to maintain labor power. Marx treats labor power like any other commodity. It is a living commodity. The value of labor power is determined by the value of the commodities it takes to keep it important.

Marx has not introduced as yet any new wrinkles. He assumes labor power is sold on the market, sold on true value. The employer does not give less in wages than the true value of labor power. There is no trickery or shortchanging.

The employer buys labor power. He hires the laborer and puts him into the factory to work. Wherever he puts him to work, the process of creating value is begun. Each hour he creates the same quantity of value. By the end of the fifth hour the value created equals the value of labor power, the value that the employer has paid in wages. The laborer produces the employer's outlay and has equaled the labor power value the employee is paid for. He is made to stay another five hours and works and creates value. This is surplus value. That is exploitation, and value created after the fifth hour is surplus. (The number of hours is merely illustrative.) The rate of surplus value is 100 percent. Surplus value equals five-fifths of 100 percent. The rate of surplus value in this illustration is 100 percent.

Capital—the machinery, plant, raw materials, and so forth used in the productive process. Capital does not contribute to surplus value. Goods, plant, and the like have value, and it is determined by the lump of labor each embodies. Capital goods do not reappear in new commodities. Labor power is capable (only) of secreting surplus value. Capital merely transfers value into a product. Profits are the result of appropriation by capitalists of surplus value. Capital has two V variable categories: (1) payroll capital V (Marx called it variable capital), variable capital for labor power—the value of capital is transferred plus surplus value; all other capital he calls (2) constant capital because value is constant, C. Variable capital makes the increase, the surplus value. C is constant, there is no change, it is inert. The relation of C to V, or C/V, Marx called the organic structure of capital. Example: In a coal mine, two-thirds of the employer's outlay is for wages and one-third for capital goods. That gives you a low organic structure of capital. In a flour mill with few workers, automatic capital is largely constant capital. There is very little variable capital. This is the high organic structure of capital. A great deal depends on the relation of the variable and the constant—it determines the structure or composition.

Commodity that is produced. Value content is C + V + Surplus Value, S.V. There are three components. One is the portion of constant capital transferred to it; part of the plant and all of the raw material in it. If it takes six months to produce a locomotive and the plant it is manufactured in will last twenty years, the part of the plant to the value of the locomotive is one-fortieth. If machine tools are used in its production and last for five years but are used six months in the manufacture, then one-tenth of the value of the tools is transferred to the locomotive. Metals are raw materials and their full value goes into the locomotive. This C is constant capital. The second component, V, is the payroll or wages expended in the building of the locomotive. The third element is surplus value. Six months: the first half day reproduces labor power (its own value); the second half day is surplus value. The locomotive is C + V + S.V. That is now the value of the commodity. All three things are composed of abstract human labor. Measuring under the three headings the same stuff results in abstract social necessary labor.

That is the Marx theory of value. However, there is more—problems. Two industries of diverse capital, for example a coal mine and a mill. It is only the variable capital that is capable of yielding surplus value. Then the product of coal will ooze with surplus value because the major portion of the capital is variable. Coal will ooze with surplus value. Bags of flour are dry because capital is constant, largely. That suggests that since surplus value profit, the rate of profit is high in coal mining but not in flour. The rate of profit should be high in coal because profit is S.V./C + V = rate of profit.

The coal mine has a high rate of profit, but the flour mill has a low rate of profit. If that is so, capitalists do not go into the flour business but rather go into the coal business. That would disturb the equilibrium; it would mean that everyone would be in coal and no one in flour. People would starve. There would be such an excess of coal mining that there would be no demand for coal. Here is what happens. Each industrialist, when he brings his product on the market, either will get +X or –X in the process of exchange (C + V + S.V.) ± X. He gets more or less of the value content. In just one place is it the same: industry where capital is even. If below or above he gets more or less on the market in order to equalize the profit. So all industries get the same rate of profit, that is, equilibrium. Equalized rate of profit for all industries regardless of their particular organic capital.

LECTURE 29
Value

Last time we considered the Marxist theory of economic equilibrium, the theory of value. Attention to following Marx like a classical economist does not identify value and price. Value to him is a fixed point on which price oscillates. Value times price. Value is a fixed point around which price vibrates. Last time I brought out what the substance is out of which value is made. It is made out of abstract labor embodied in commodities exchanged on the market. Abstract labor of which a lump of a particular size in commodities is measured by the length of time to produce the commodity under standard conditions. The commodity on the market represents a lump of congealed labor. That in turn is broken down into three parts, depending upon the origin. Value = C + V + S.V. Each commodity contains a share of constant capital—planned machinery and raw material plus the variable capital, which is the payroll expenditure for the commodity, plus surplus value, which is the result of exploitations—the result of institutional power of the employer to force the employee to work a number of hours beyond what is needed to produce power. If value is determined by formula, then the different industries depend on organic capital. the coal industry with a lot of payroll capital is the only one which sprouts surplus value. This would find everyone in the coal industry. Contrast this with the flour industry which is dry (surplus value content); coal is wet (surplus value). If the formula represented the actual situation then there would be disorder in industry. You would have a ticklish market situation. The result would be too much coal (price below value) on the market but not enough flour (price above its value).

That does not happen because of one industry but because of the permanent deflection on the market around a fixed point X where price vibrates. Permanent deflection from the formula varies depending on the organic capital of the industry in question. If the industry averages between the constant and variable capital then the formula holds. If the industry is above or below then on the market the capitalist of the industry will either be robbed by others or he robs. You have the notion of a redistribution or secondary distribution of surplus value. Surplus value is appropriated by the capitalists. The other process is that each does his own and then they divide up. That is what Marx says: +X or –X. each capitalist gets enough to enable them all to get a *uniform rate of profit.* The source of profit surplus value and profit is computed on the basis of constant and variable capital. There is a tendency for all industries to realize an average rate of profit. An average rate of profit is brought about by competition. The value the capitalist realizes in the market—value shaved off because otherwise too high a profit or value is added to from shavings to give him an average rate of profit by others—this is caused by competition on the market. This introduces an amendment to the original theory. Now you have permanent deflection by addition or subtraction of X, which depends on the structure of the capital.

Price vibrates, but it is only in rare instances that price vibrates around value. In the majority of industries price vibrates around (C + V + S.V.) ± X, which is Production Price. Marx was not concerned with demand and supply changing. He was concerned with the level of the ocean. First he formulated the level C + V + S.V. and then amended it to come out with an average rate of profit by addition of ±X.[1]

Contradiction of people if Marx changed his idea. The adding of X or shavings of the other fellows' surplus value or minus value is just like friction. I do not believe an attack on Marx is repudiating oneself.

Theory of equilibrium: It is in the producing of an average rate of profit. Marx's equilibrium is not much concerned with vibrations but with fixed points.

PART II OF THE SYSTEM: DYNAMIC THEORY OF CAPITALISM

Source of profit—surplus value—exploitation of labor and an average rate of profit.

No capitalist is satisfied with an average rate of profit. He gets profit above the average. He gets it by pioneering in industrial technology, by introducing more efficient machinery. Capitalist A pioneers and runs ahead of other capitalists and introduces more effective machinery—so long as he outdistances the pack—the conditions that the dominant majority determines as social labor necessary. So the pioneer capitalist, if he manages to cut down the labor time used in production of his product, then is a gainer because as yet the representative type of production is not his but something less efficient. That is how he realizes super profits, by running ahead of the pack. How does he do it? He does it by increasing his investment for machinery and his plant. He increases the constant capital at the expense of variable capital. More machinery is brought in than labor. By and by the remainder of the capitalists begin to work to bring about the same result. They increase the ratio of constant capital to the variable and put in better machinery. Then the value of the product drops because what was exceptional now is representative. Capitalist A's record becomes common. The value of the product has been reduced because the social necessary labor time to produce has been reduced. There has taken place a general increase of constant capital over variable capital. Since variable capital is the only one to sprout surplus value the result is the lowering of the rate of profit. What started as a hopeful adventure for a single capitalist has turned out to be a sorry experience for the whole gang. Others follow suit and when all have the same efficiency, there is no additional surplus value. They really reduced their own rate of profit. They have striven and gotten what? It is only temporary and only the pioneer gets extra profits. There are ways of defeating

1. Rate of profit = $\dfrac{\text{S. V.}}{\text{C} + \text{V}}$

this falling rate of profit. Marx said this is an important feature of the capitalist system: *tendency of the rate of profit to fall.* It is a phenomenon which begins counter-measures, and capitalists try to defeat it. How to arrest it? Some of it comes about as a by-product of the whole competitive process. The capitalistic system is on its toes and improves the means of production. It also means industries that produce consumer goods. The result thereby lowers the value of labor power. If commodities are subject to technological improvement the time to produce goes down. Therefore labor power goes down. Five hours for the laborer to recompense the employer for wages may be reduced to three or four hours. Surplus value beyond on five hours now is seven hours. It would mean three and seven rather than five and five. Automatic by-product. This adds to the surplus value—seven hours against three hours. This is a slowing up of the formula's rate of profit. More surplus value out of labor power. This is not enough; it is a by-product resulting in arrest. It is supplemented by conscious policies. First speed up the driving process; compress the pores of labor time. The sweatshop stroke is driven. That shortens the life of the worker but the capitalist does not care. That is one way to obtain surplus value. Another way is to short-change the laborer on the labor market. Employers combine and depress it below the value of labor power. It is the other form of counteracting the fall of the rate of profit. The last method that comes in the latter days of capitalism is imperialism. Export capital to a colonial country which you dominate and force the population to work for less than labor power and exploit the consumers of the colony. That leads to war.

STRUCTURAL CHANGE IN CAPITALISM

Changes have been made in the competitive process that operates, bringing about the fall in the rate of profit and begetting endeavors to counteract the fall. What are the structural changes that result from competition and exploitation? One change is the squeezing out of the middle class. A concentration of capital. The other thing is the increase in the misery of labor. The result of heightened technological development is that the demand for labor falls and there is a reserve army of the unemployed. Wage earners are employed sporadically. They are employed during prosperity. Normally there is no demand for them. The capitalist is unable to give full employment. The unemployed affect the wages of the employed by pulling wages down. Therefore there is an increase in the misery of labor. This drives labor to revolution.

Trade unionism can do something to arrest this, but not enough. Trade unionism can prevent the short-changing of labor on the market, or can do so when industry is prosperous or expands. The role assigned to trade unionism is education. The mass of wage earners are taught Marxism. This is brought in by the trade union as a protector. It is not adequate, but it helps temporarily and brings in the movement, and thus an advance is made for Marxism.

The third change in capitalism which works to bring on revolution is the phenomenon of depression and crisis. Marx has several forces operating to make crisis inevitable and of long duration. One force is the downward pressure on wages which is the result of the unemployed. The purchasing power of the consumers goes down in proportion to the production power.

There is a growing disparity between productive capacity and effective consuming capacity. That is one factor tending to bring about crisis. The other is the whole planlessness of the capitalistic system. There is no central plan. Anarchy in production. The market is the regulator and it is poor. Some industries expand but they overexpand. When they overexpand they are inflated and ready to topple. There is a planlessness of production and it is aggravated by the fact that there are two categories of industries—consumer and producer. Producer-goods industries pay wages and they purchase commodities. The two kinds of industries must mesh. Respective expansion must be harmonious, but in view of the planlessness such harmonious expansion can be only by sheer accident. Harmonious meshing in of two kinds of industries.

All these factors—the growing disparity between productive capacity and effective consuming capacity, planlessness, and misery—tend to bring about depression and crisis. It gets worse and worse as time goes on. The capitalist system becomes desperate and gets a new lease on life only by imperialism, which means war. Capitalism is weakened socially by its own devouring of the middle class and the proletariat grows as a result of capitalistic expansion. The proletariat is the grave-digger of capitalism.

The economics and politics of Marx mesh. It is like theology. You cannot prove or disprove it. Modern socialists do not stress it.

DISCUSSIONS

Miscellaneous Topics Developed in Discussions

DISCUSSION 1
The Significance of Job Consciousness

In my book, *A Theory of the Labor Movement,* I formulated a theory of the labor movement and economic institutions. It is historical and theoretical. The crux of the theory is that social or labor movements here are different from those initiated by intellectuals. Where the labor movement was permitted to develop freely without legal restraints, such as trade unions on their own, a new leadership sprang forth—it differed from the mentality of the intellectuals. There was a struggle between the intellectuals and the trade unionist concept. Usually the trade unionist concept won out.

There was only one country where the intellectual won out and it was in Russia. This was due to the fact that it issued from a different historical mode. Russia had one thousand years of history and it had not experienced certain stages in its development that the western countries experienced, such as that of the guild system. The guilds were the cradle of the middle class, and out of the guilds business grew—and grew as an independent body. It was independent of government; in fact, it was a partner of government. Russia never had such an independent development. Russia never had a real feudalism. The Russian nobility was humble, a group servile to the ruler. Russia had peasants until 1930 and ownership was collective and not individual. During the first years after the Bolshevist Revolution the peasants were permitted to universalize ownership.

Russia proved to be a passive community in the hands of the revolutionaries. Russian history had not given to Russia the center of resistance to revolution from the left. In other countries there was resistance—thus Communism failed.

Western society and communities were immune from attack from the left largely due to normal development of the middle class, trade unions, et cetera; and this was absent from Russia. This I call job consciousness. It is the theory of labor movement that considers the job movement.

I am going to read an article that will appear in the *New Leader.* This is a paper which is the official organ of the old line Socialists who broke from the Socialists under Norman Thomas—the Trade Union Socialists. This paper is a haven of refuge for Max Eastman and others who engaged in revolutionary activities, but became disillusioned. Refugees are also writing in the paper. The editor, Dr. William E. Bohn, asked me to write an article on "The Passing of Job Consciousness." [Perlman read his article. The excerpts given here are from the article as published.]

> The assailants of America's job-conscious unionism, from DeLeon's day to our own, have consistently viewed it as a phenomenon in labor movement pathology. To the extreme left, job-consciousness is a case of a hopeless degeneration of vital tissue; to the "centrists" and the rightists, an arrested development to be overcome by suitable ideological injections. Although the racketeer-infested segment of American unionism bears out the former, and the unhappy performance of the AFL leadership in 1935–36 which gave us the civil war in labor may fairly be cited in proof of the latter, to the writer job-consciousness is primarily an emphasis on what is *nuclear,* what is the central core of labor's interest, which, when uncomplicated by personalities, passion and dogmatism, itself compels a widening of the area of interest, *with changing conditions.* On the other hand, American labor history teaches us that nuclear it must remain if the movement is not to weaken or disintegrate. . . .
>
> But first we must explain how American job-consciousness came to be. The Gompersian program was the product of a half century's effort by the American labor movement to attain stability and a real foothold. The struggling unions had to learn to cut the cord that tied them to the farmer and other middle class anti-monopoly movements, with which they shared an overweening passion for self-employment and a burning faith in salvation through political parties thrust up by the "producing classes." Labor had to learn to avoid these enthusiasms and "sure" paths to victory and to concentrate on the *job* interest as the only hard reality in the wage earner's life. Labor's historical experimenting also extended to the American community as a whole, the "public," to the employers and to the government.
>
> It learned that an attack, or even what might be misconstrued as an intended attack, on private property and enterprise as institutions would only be a free gift to its enemies; that employers, if the gods were willing, could be coerced or sometimes cajoled into a joint job administration under a trade agreement; that the structure of political action in the United States doomed a labor party setting up in com-

petition with the "old" parties but opened a possibility for carrying collective bargaining into politics and even for infiltration of the old parties; and finally, that the American government with its states' rights, judicial review and general checks and balances was a very limited instrument for labor's good and often a menace to be warded off (for example, the Sherman Act). But if the government of the land was to be handled with caution and fear, labor could still go ahead building up two kinds of unofficial governments, each around the job interest.

One was a government for the labor movement itself; erected on the principle of exclusive union jurisdiction and setting up the labor movement as a job empire with affiliated job kingdoms, duchies and baronies (*Nulle terre sans seigneur!*) and held together through the absolute and pitiless suppression of "dual" or illegitimate unions. The other kind of government, dealing as it did with the conditions of employment, had to reckon with the employers, but under it the unions sought, wherever possible, full possession of the "job territory" through the closed or union shop.

Such was American unionism when the sovereignty of American government was confronted with the stronger sovereignty of American business; when the economic system including job opportunities was being kept up and expanded by private enterprise alone. Under these circumstances, labor's task was clearly to build its union fortifications over the several job territories, mostly craft, a few covering an industry. Unionism of that period saw little lying outside the immediate economic area that could either improve the conditions of the job or multiply job opportunities.

The great changes which have recently been compelling job-conscious unionism to raise its sights to take in a new and vast job hinterland, to remove many of the boundaries within its own job empire, and to supplement economic action with politico-legislative action, have occurred in the economic system as a whole, in technology and in government. . . .

American unionism will progress not by an ideological "conversion" which will expunge job-consciousness but as an organic reinterpretation of job-conscious unionism to make it fit the new environment as the Gompers version fitted the old. For, in the last analysis, job-consciousness is not a state of progressive anaesthesia but one of never failing sensitiveness—the very manifestation of life in the wage earners and their movements.[1]

I contend that job consciousness is the nucleus in labor interest. The editor's idea is that labor is interested in things beyond jobs, its job consciousness is

1. Selig Perlman, "Growing Role of Government as Creator of Jobs, Need for Political Strength, Dooms 'Pure and Simple' Unionism," *New Leader*, February 28, 1942, p. 4.

dead. I say job consciousness is necessary as a nucleus. In labor today job interest can be defended only if the hinterland around it is taken care of.

Contrasting approaches are that the intellectual in the labor movement starts with the theory of the political shaping society and looks to the labor movement. So far it did not do it, so I make an injection. So do not confine yourself just to job interest but to the wider view—society.

I believe the labor movement (union) is trying to find an anchorage in the American environment. To find a foothold it hit on job interest as the thing to tie workers together. Thus no matter what your religion, et cetera, if a wage earner, you have certain interests common to other earners and you get them through unions. That is the procedure of the American labor movement— organization around the job.

American political parties are so flexible and clever that labor cannot get ahead in politics, so it decided to keep out of politics. The early unionism in America that Gompers founded stuck to jobs. As far as the job is concerned it did two things. (1) It organized the union movement[2]—job empire—this was the A.F.L. and it protected them against other organizations coming in. (2) Also conditions of employment and therein took into consideration the organization of employers. There was the closed shop or union shop. The demand for it is rising. The push for it will continue. That was the unionism that developed when the American government was weak under checks and balances. That was when the union members learned they could not compete against the politicians.

I feel *job consciousness* interest still remains. But the leadership of labor has learned, with the New Deal, that the American environment has changed—the American government is now in one piece. The American government has competence over the labor conditions in the country. The American government has become centralized as far as labor relations are concerned. The government was formerly a broken link to lean upon but now it is a strong support. Labor's job consciousness forces it to go into politics; and the pioneers in that area are the railroad unions. The railway industry has been under government control since 1906. Thus the railroad unions went into politics and have an effective lobby. Job interest took them into the field—thus politics. Now all industry is subject to the federal government under the new system of government.

Pure and simple unionism is dead because of job interests; labor goes far afield in politics and legislation. That does not mean that labor organization is a political party. The government has changed but the way we control the government has not changed. Labor gets the most out of the government by allying itself with humanitarian political interests.

Labor impelled by job consciousness has been driven into the legislative field. I look upon it as labor unions struggling for survival, and they are mindful of

2. The type organized around the job.

changes in the environment. Here then is the expansion of interest in the labor movement.

The other approach is the process of history—it stems from Marxism: the proletarian—he is to take over society. The proletarian is not doing the right thing; he is monkeying with unionism.

In Great Britain now the intellectual Laski wants to socialize industry, but labor does not follow because it knows Great Britain is fighting for its life and thus there is a need for national unity. There is controversy in Great Britain. It is Bevin (trade unionist—a socialist) versus Laski. Bevin says let us have a socialistic England, but he is not in a hurry. He is concerned with the aim of democratizing England but without orienting itself to the star of socialization. Laski says now is the time to socialize England and take over big industries. To him this war is an opportunity to put over that thing.

To trade unionism it is essential to fortify trade unions by digging in—entering politics, and so on. To have control—control over the job.

This is approaching something from two places. One looks at it from a plan, a blueprint—it is abstract and the people are instruments, a means to an end. The other approach is to take people as human and look at everything from a burning concern—the *job*. Even the most job-conscious movement is not just materialistic but idealistic too. The average man wants to have rights. To have his dignity protected—the right to a job—not to be pushed around, etc.

My idea is that the democratic cause hauls in the concrete human being and he has rights and is just as good as anyone else. You have unions so you are not pushed around. The fear of interest varies and depends on conditions. When the government is controlling the hinterland of the job fortress, then he builds. The real or center of concern is the *concrete human with concrete aspirations* and the rest is just instruments to that end. Thus it is more democratic.

That is what I call *job conscious unionism* and it is dynamic.[3]

DISCUSSION NOTE: At this meeting Marx's *The Communist Manifesto* and Lenin's *State and Revolution* were assigned for reading and future discussion. Professor Perlman's own book, *A Theory of the Labor Movement,* was to be read during the course of the semester. Professor Perlman noted that current events would get attention in the course, particularly those that contributed to the general theory of social movements.

3. For further observation and thought of Perlman, see Selig Perlman, "What's Wrong in American Labor?" *New Leader*, June 5, 1943; Selig Perlman, "Can Labor and the Professors Work Together?" *New Leader*, September 4, 1943.

DISCUSSION 2
"The Communist Manifesto" and Marx's
Interpretation of History
  A Contrast with Charles Beard's Interpretation
  Ideals in the Marxist Interpretation
  The Significance of Productive Forces
  The Ruling Class

There are two aspects of Marxism. The first aspect is the concept of history, including the formulation of the dynamics of the structure of capitalism, and revolutionary politics, which is only one part of the Marxist system of thought. I am leaving out the second aspect, the economic theory of Marxism, including the Marxist theory of economic equilibrium and the other part of economic theory, which is economic dynamics. We will take up the side of economic theory later.

The author of *What Marx Really Meant*, G. D. H. Cole, is an Oxford Professor and economic advisor of the British Labor Party. His book is a restatement of Marxist theory—from the standpoint of a living Marxist. It is written as though he is a contemporary of ours and one who continued to formulate theory. It is a valuable book and will be discussed later.

Today we will turn to the *Communist Manifesto*. Until 1904 and 1905 there was heavy censorship in Russia. It was lifted for a while, so the smaller works of Marx and Engels were able to be published. I was a student and saw the *Manifesto* in the window under a different title. It was called *A Philosophy of History*. This was due to censorship.

When you attempt to formulate a philosophy or science of history, would you be inclined to feature spectacular events of history for a science of history? try to get away from the unique aspect of history? look for objective forces rather than individuals? Where did Marx look for objective driving forces? In economic forces. Beard looked to the Constitution and stated an economic interpretation of the Constitution.[1] A Marxist is an activist. According to Marx men made history—it did not make itself.

My point is, the economic interpretation of history is much narrower than the Marxist interpretation of history because the Marxist way explains religious and idealistic movements. Marx says ideas are not from heaven, but ideals are shaped by material reality. It is not necessary to point out that the majority of the people at the United States Convention of the Constitution did not have personal wealth. Marx said that fifty-seven of the people were free, wholly uncommitted in their purpose of benefiting the nation, but that the concrete formation of their ideal was taken from the interest in the class to which they belonged. Everyone could have held the theory of social welfare, without personal award, but the criterion they used as to what is good for the

1. Charles Beard, *An Economic Interpretation of the Constitution* (New York: Macmillan Co., 1913).

country, or welfare for the country—that was shaped by the class interest of the ruling class.

Distinction. There is a distinction between an economic interpretation of history and the Marxist interpretation. With the economic way one ends up with racketeers. Marx has a realistic conception of history. I think Beard's step is a regression from Marx and it prevented the public from thinking realistically. In Marxism there is all the room you want for personal idealism. Ideals arise from materials. Idealists are not impelled by relief motives, but the ideals they profess are shaped by the stage of material development at the time. Ideals were shaped in terms of giving the widest scope of action to the rising commercial class. At a different period—idealists of today would have ideals shaped by the interest of the proletariat. Marx's interpretation is a realist's interpretation. The idea gained from Beard is that everyone was engaged in a racket. Marx has a materialistic interpretation of history. He willingly accepts ideals—the force of ideals to move the human—but believes ideals are shaped by the material conditions of the day and especially by the interest of the progressive class of the day. To Marx, ideals such as justice or freedom are relative to a particular period in society. He scoffed at permanent, timeless ideals. To him ideals were derived from the necessities and essentials of the time.

The Marxist intellectual mechanism of the theory of history is to see if there is a common pattern. Darwin had the law of the motion of life, Marx the law of the motion of the history of human beings. The intellectual pattern of Darwinism (mechanicism), of *The Origin of Species*,[2] is organism and environment. Life manifests itself through variation—endless variation. Environment sits in judgment and eliminates the unfit. The factor Marx points out—variation—goes on and on in productive forces. It is without plan—spontaneous—it just takes place. The idea is that humans forever are trying to economize efforts and get the best results possible—that is the basic thing in Marx, just as variation is in Darwin. The accretion of productive forces—you can prove that some periods are slow and some are faster. There is capitalist institutional hindrance to the accretion of forces. However, you cannot stop the accretion of productive forces.

Productive forces are subject to accretion. Moreover productive forces are handled by humans—they exist in and through humans (the minds of humans). In Marx's concept productive forces are worked by humans and within humans and then go on—a perpetual process of accretion. In the process of production we have a basic differentiation of humans, that is, their function. Those who plan and discharge, and on the other side those who execute orders. The managerial function and the executive side. In the joint process of handling productive forces there is a basic differentiation. The managerial side—the ruling class—and the other class is the subject class.

2. Charles Darwin, *On the Origin of Species by Means of Natural Selection* (London: J. Murray, 1859).

There is a basic human differentiation within the productive process, and from that class division stems. That means production relations. We must admit the influence of law—property and ownership must come in. In a communist society you could have functional differentiation without the rise of classes and without private ownership. In class societies there are classes which exclude modern socialism and primitive communism. The Marxist idea is one of excluding primitive communism and socialism; in between you have class societies and there the institution of property gives shape to productive relations. The managerial group derives its mandate to manage from property rights enforced by the state: institutions, law, government, and so forth.

The accretion of productive forces forever changes the production relations. Relations function effectively if they are outside the support of property and control of government.

The tribunal that decides the fitness or unfitness, which decides for elimination or continuation, of the ruling class is the tribunal of productive forces. A ruling class rides into power because at the time it is the most adept at handling the productive forces and it gives the widest scope. By and by productive forces go on and the time comes when the institutional framework begins to act as a straitjacket for the forces. The institutional framework does not stretch—it is cast iron—it does not stretch but it breaks, and that is the same as social revolution. There are two aspects of the event—a nonhuman and human aspect. The nonhuman—abstractions, forces, and a jacket. The human side gives a picture of a class struggle—the progressive class and a reactionary class, which has begun to be a hindrance to the forces and whose institutionalism is a straitjacket.

One speaks of forces and the institutional framework of society. When we think in terms of humans, then we think of two classes. One as reactionary, with institutions acting as a straitjacket, and the other progressive, with institutions like a roomy house, where the productive forces find plenty of room.

There are two kinds of historical periods—one critical and the other organic. I have just described the critical period when forces are hemmed in. The human side means a social revolution.

We have productive forces and the institutional setup of the old ruling class and the new ruling class. What decides the outcome is the pressure of the productive forces upon the institutional framework. The theory is different than in Darwinism. There the outside environment sits in judgment and kills the unfit. There we see the end of life. In Darwin the environment judges. But here productive forces sit in judgment; they determine which class is fit to rule—and this occurs in the critical period. History is of two periods—critical and organic.

In the Marxist conception—historical periods—housing forces could grow. On the human side it meant a period such as the first half of the nineteenth century when the capitalistic class reached power and put through an institutional structure favorable to productive forces. Then later the housing deteriorates and the symptom is depression and the crisis of 1857. That is the beginning. The productive forces and the institutional setup conflict, and on the human side the capitalist class is fearful and looks back. We have the rise of a new class, the proletariat. Its first manifestations are timid, but it grows in confidence and self-estimation. That is why Marx pounced on the Commune, because for him it was the fulfillment of a prophecy. The first symptom of the proletariat class action was earlier—the strike of the silk workers in Lyons, France. Soldiers were sent to put the strike down. That was the first time that Marx knew the baby would live. The Chartist movement he thought of as a worker movement. Then there was 1848.[3] To him the Commune of 1871 was a wonderful thing.[4]

DISCUSSION NOTE: Assigned readings were V. I. Lenin, *Imperialism: The Highest Stage of Capitalism;* G. D. H. Cole, *What Marx Really Meant.*

DISCUSSION 3
The Origin of Political Power,
Marx's Theory and Others
   The Phenomenon of Nazism
   Some Comments on James Burnham's
   "Managerial Revolution"
   The New Deal State

ETHICS IN THE MATERIALISTIC CONCEPT OF HISTORY

There is room for individual ethics and idealism in Marxism. Whether the ethical factor is of independent origin or due to material—this can be argued. Marx recognizes the ethic propensity in the human, but the stuff out of which the ideal is made is the material condition of life.

Today we will discuss *the political theory of Marxism.* The origin of political power. First of all, I will discuss the materialist conception of history and then I will apply criticism.

Marx. The orthodox theory of the origin of political power throughout history—the source of political power of formation—in Marxism, is from the ruling class. It is the nucleus of the state. From the ruling class the state is shaped and controlled and used.

3. The Chartist Movement in England sought reforms in favor of the workers after their disappointment with the Reform Bill of 1832. In 1838 the people drew up a People's Charter embodying six demands for reform which became known as the points of Chartism, but it failed to be adopted. In 1848 the Chartist Movement reached its climax and then collapsed. Parliament rejected the Chartist demands, and the resulting disorders were easily put down.
4. The revolutionary French government which ruled in Paris, March-May 1871.

Other theories of the origin of political power: American. The conventional American theory—the consent of the governed, and the governed, also, are sovereign. There is a popular sovereign (the voters). The human being has the right to vote. The sovereign is the people, and it is an undifferentiated sovereign—no classes—and all vote. There are geographical constituents comprising people of all sorts. The American theory is that the government is the instrument of undifferentiated people, and they are out to realize the general good and carry out the general will.

Divine. Divine right—ruler through God. Stronger if rule by God and also the head of religion. For example, Byzantine under Justinian, who really was both ruler and pope.

Hegel. Hegelian theory—the state is the highest incarnation of God. The general theory of history is that the absolute spirit is unfolding. The absolute spirit expresses itself through leading nations—such as Greece. The basic process of history is the unfolding of the absolute spirit through the succession of nations.

Oppenheimer. Oppenheimer—the conquest theory. The source of power formation was not the economic function of managing productive forces, but from conquest—sheer physical power. If you possess political power, then you can dominate the economic. An example is military ability—conquer and rule. *Military theory*—not just military power but power of the government too. The Turks have shown it too. *Conquest or political theory of state*—foreign conqueror from the outside. The internal conqueror that does not spring from the economic. Internal conquerors are proficient in fighting and wire-pulling. Do we have phenomena in our own day that can get more light from the Oppenheimer theory of conquest than from the Marxist theory?

How did or would Marx explain the Nazis or the Fascists? They are the last stand of capitalism. With the rise of the labor movement, and with the strength manifested by the labor movement as expressed in the social service of the state (social insurance, welfare payments, and so on) under democracy—that is manifest—then the democratic guarantees are withdrawn in favor of a dictatorial regime that would smash the unions and take away the right to strike.

A friend of mine under the influence of Laski believed the New Deal in the United States was the beginning of the withdrawing of civil liberties. That it was going toward a capitalistic dictatorship. I did not agree with him.

To a Marxist a regime without some economic class is inconceivable. It is inconceivable to think of political phenomena of government in action unless some economic class, for example, is its very heart. In the Marxist concept a government is invariably the mouthpiece—the executive organization—of the economic class. Some Marxists point out the exception—Trotsky did—such as when economic classes balance each other. Then men on horseback dominate. There is an equilibrium between economic classes and it is a vacuum, and then a pure military leader comes in and rules. Trotsky went on to say it cannot go on forever. Classes are progressively getting out of equal weight. Then they crack up, too, and then there is revolution. He saw the brief period where economic classes do not play the main actions—an outsider comes in.

But still, normally, to Marxism the heart of the phenomena of political power is that there must be a functioning economic class. That is the materialistic, or economic, interpretation of political power of formation.

As I see the Nazi phenomenon—in this connection as political phenomenon and in power formation and wielding—I deviate from the Marxist theory of political formation.[1] If a country is subject to a number of critical situations that affect the middle classes—as inflation in addition to the rise of organized labor—at the same time, you have the following. Inflation: the middle-class loses its savings, there is further development of big business that impinges upon small business, and big business is represented by the Jews. The rise of organized labor: to the middle class the Social Democrats and organized labor are the scum of the earth. After the war, laborers organized politically and there were trade unions and they held state offices and received great protection in the form of labor legislation. That hurt—to the middle class it was adding insult to injury. An emotional reaction to a social revolution was taking place. A transposition of the classes takes place—the lower classes have risen and the former higher classes have gone down. This was aggravated by more economic depression. And the children of the middle class have no prospect— they have no function. Mixed in with that is national humiliation. Army officers were reduced to poverty. They were dissatisfied and lost prestige. Then there was a movement which addressed itself to the middle class; it knew how to pick its grievances, and played on their envy. The leadership itself was of the middle class and had their mentality, and it had strong nationalism. The leaders were of the same social group as the middle class; they were skillful, and knew how to act as an internal conqueror, and take advantage of the existing discontents and put themselves forth as a savior. This is a middle-class movement—plebeian.

Then they approached the big businessmen and the junkers (estate owners) and made them believe they are young men with their hearts in the right place. Some of the businessmen thought that the fellows were effective and we need them and we will be able to control. Thus they were allies and in the end got into power. Once in power they waited and then extended their power. The unions were immediately smashed, and then they took the churches. Their people take over some business. They do not have a definite social policy—it is flexible. They are committed only to stay in power. Aside from that, they go to the right and then to the left. They kill people who are radical, then crack down on the corporations. They become rich and build fortunes at the same time. How about the middle classes? They got little—certain men get a lot.

1. A description follows of Germany after World War I.

The middle class is not benefited as such; it just contributed a new human array to the seat of power. The new rulers had a source of strength like the Mongols—great politicians and warriors. They had the qualifications of conquerors. A political military formation. We have then a political phenomenon about which the Marxists say—capitalists are there. They cling to this to save their formula. I think the popular criticism is not based on, Who owns what? but rather, Who makes the most important decisions? and, When a man gets wealthy, does he get so because it is from industry or because of political power and he grabs?

To me the Nazi phenomenon is one of power formation—better explained by Oppenheimer than Marx. The dynamic factor is not economic but military. Power does not stem from economics. Here is the issue—the difference between an economic interpretation of political formation and a looser interpretation.

Different periods in human history show that there is a difference in political power formation. In the nineteenth century, political power came from economic roots. There was a contraction of the government and an exaltation of private enterprise. In our own day we have reverted. Economic expansion is over and we struggle with chronic depression; that brings government back into the picture.

The nineteenth century was an exceptional century—economic expansion and government contraction. Marxism reflects the nineteenth century. It is a nineteenth-century product, and the emphasis Marx places on economics reflects the nineteenth century. With the period of rapid expansion there was a reversal—economics ceased to be the central song; there was a return of the political phenomenon and the question was, Who personifies the political power? Will it be the humanitarian, as in the United States, or the modern Mongol and his use of political expertness and the extension of himself over the map? They got there because they grabbed the previous political power and because they had a proficient military formation.

Recently there has been a big discussion over the book by James Burnham, *The Managerial Revolution.*[2] Burnham bunches together Russia and Germany as the same thing—supreme managers (supreme management). My reply to him is that he overlooks ownership. Among the old capitalists some were deprived of ownership, but others retained it, and new ones came in. So my criticism of Burnham is that he underestimates ownership.

To my way of thinking management—the managerial revolution—is a phase, nor am I impressed so much by ownership. *But how come ownership? Who gives a man ownership?* Is it by political entrenchment? What about the chances of hanging on to it? I am not impressed by management as supreme nor by ownership. I take the dynamic side. How did it get there and what are its chances of staying there?

Different periods in history bring forth different groupings in society that are makers of history. In the nineteenth century it was the economic classes.

2. James Burnham, *The Managerial Revolution* (New York: John Day Co., Inc., 1941).

Before the nineteenth century it was dynasties. Now we are getting back to
those who can organize conquests, external and internal, and seize political
power and permeate the economic groupings. *The source of strength is not
the economic function but the military or political function.*

Today it is easy to determine which is the ruling class. Who decides to go to
war? (The finance capitalist did not encourage war—thus he does not really
rule.)

A book I read said the Nazi is sent into the business corporation and gets
the salaries and thus the business corporation rules the Nazi—*this is silly.* The
book, by James Burnham—*The Managerial Revolution*—caused a lot of talk. I
think it is not a managerial revolution that is the issue, but the organization of
political power. The internal conqueror is a politician. A gambler plays for a
big strike. Goering is at the top because he is a ruthless fellow and is clever. He
is a politician.

In the nineteenth century there was economic expansion and the economic
industrialist arose. Then there were barriers to the flow of goods. The social
situation changed. Then the inherent dangers formerly held in check did not
operate and there was a radical change in the social situation. Then a depression, and the government had to come in and hold up the tottering system. It
failed and it toppled and then we have what we have today. Emphasis is on
the social situations—offer to the people to come to the front. An environ-
mental interpretation, but still I try to keep the human in the center.

Today we have a new phenomenon—not an economic phenomenon. It is a
political military phenomenon—the modern Mongol theory of the state.

How can we describe the New Deal state? It is a phenomenon of agglomera-
tion. A political leadership which at the same time is playing essential camps
in our own country. The South gets capital and does so by keeping down the
labor standards; thus you have an influx of capital from the North. To keep
the South in line, Roosevelt bribes it. Instead of capital from the North as an
influx, he pumps capital into the South—a pipeline—boosts prices, the T.V.A.,
public improvements, and so on.

A dynamic leadership that knows how to satisfy all—that is how Roosevelt
maintains leadership. Three months ago he almost lost the leadership of Congress (Lewis[3]—strikes, and so on). Congress rebelled and we had the Smith
bill. Then the Japanese—and no longer did the President have to cater to the
South and the Smith bill was put in storage.

It is a pragmatic state. (A state that does not operate on a particular theory.)
It has ideals, but on the instrumental side it is flexible.

In the year 1938 Roosevelt was defeated in his attempt to purge, to defeat,
certain congressmen—George of Georgia, Tydings of Maryland, and others. It
was a purge of his own party and he was defeated. The country was in a reactionary mood. He came back afterwards due to the war situation.

3. John L. Lewis (1880-1969), well-known American labor leader, who served as president of the United Mine Workers of America, 1920-60.

DISCUSSION 4
*Marx's Theory of Truth and
Human Nature*
   The Utopians and Marx
   *Some Comments on Cole's
   "What Marx Really Meant"*

You have asked if there was a more direct answer or explanation by Marx of
the proletariat dictatorship to a classless society; isn't there the danger of a
bureaucracy or a class and, thus, not really a classless society?

Marx and his group got away from the Utopian Socialists who were great
blueprinters; the Marxists were concerned with movements and actual things.
They did not bother telling too much of the future. When the future is here
it will work out. Marx deals with the capitalist class struggle and the stress on
the movement. There is not so much theorizing.

The first stage is the efficiency wage (private income). The second stage (the
final stage) is each produces according to his ability and he gets what he needs.

Lenin was not a clear thinker, but he had hunches. His contributions in
1902–8 were that the political party was to be a party of professional revolutionists. This fitted Russia.

Trotsky was at the height of his prestige in the 1920s. Then he was going off
into the clouds. He advocated the conscription of labor. Lenin saw that he was
crazy. He said give the peasants an inducement to improve their economic
position. This was the policy that was used. For a while it looked as though
the peasant would be like the American farmer.

Marx was a developmentalist—the unfolding process of history. Reason as
such had no potency, but class interests had potency—that is why the Utopians
were not getting anywhere. Marx said there is no such thing as a rational tribunal. Marx got his developmental idea from Hegel—the notion of stages and so
on. The Marxist developmental type of reasoning was strong and revolutionary.

To the eighteenth-century rationalist there was only one truth. The way to
discover truth was to throw away the prejudices of the past. Marx discovers
truth by searching for it—humans view it through the spectacles of interests of
the class. During the progressive stage of the life cycle ... as the class regresses
it veils the truth more and more, and then it turns away from the truth. According to the Marxist theory of truth-finding you do not find it just by dis-
carding the prejudices. The degree to which truth is veiled from the truth-seeker
of a class varies. While the class is progressive the veil is thin. Marx looked on
himself as one who had changed classes. He was a bourgeois and went to the
proletariat class. He was the truth-seeker for the proletariat, and since the proletariat was not interested in perpetuating class power for the future he had no

reason to see the truth veiled. Hence, the proletariat truth-seekers could see the naked truth.

Utopians like Fourier[1] discover the inner drives of a human being. (Max Eastman[2] finds salvation in psychology and gives up socialism.) Fourier discusses the permanent stable traits of nature. He wanted to devise a social order in conformity with these inner urges. He believes labor is repulsive only because the social and productive forces cut across the natural instincts of human beings. Human nature is a bundle of instincts. Fourier said map out the instincts and then reorganize society and people will be happy.

Robert Owen[3] believed human nature is the product of environment, and that is why he condemned institutions—because they played havoc with human nature. He came to the United States and bought land. He expected to have a harmonious society. He did not quite get a harmonious society, and said it was because already it was not of the shape of the people. Thus his plan of education—take the children away from their parents.

Marx's theory of human nature. His assumption is that human nature is not fixed and can be molded by institutions. But institutions are subject to a particular sequence (feudal, capitalistic, and so on). Human nature is plastic. Marx's notion is that human nature is like colored cubes—cubes that can be taken and put into a pattern. Institutions shift about the pattern. We have human propensities, but they do not determine—they are just raw material. Social orders change in a certain sequence—the materialistic conception of history. Under each order a remolding of human nature. Adam Smith's theory is that it is natural to humans to trade and to barter. Marx said it is not natural to humans as such but natural to capitalists to trade and barter. Here again we see the contrast of Marx with an outstanding Utopian like Fourier.

The productive force is really human culture, especially on the technical side. The productive forces are in the human mind—the product of the human mind. Darwin: the environment sits in judgment on life. Marx: the productive forces sit in judgment on institutions. To Darwin what is external sits on life, and to Marx what is life sits on the external.

Productive forces—the Marxist concept. There are two divisions of the human mind—technical (that is, the productive forces) and institutions (the organization of society). The time comes when the productive forces clash with the institutions—which you might call the ordering powers of the mind. There is a clash between the two divisions of the human mind—the technical and social

1. Charles Fourier (1772-1837), French social reformer, advocated a utopian society based on the voluntary association of producers in units known as phalanxes.

2. Max Eastman, editor of *The Masses*, 1913-17; *The Liberator*, 1918-22; roving editor for *Reader's Digest* from 1941 until his death in 1969.

3. Robert Owen (1771-1858), British reformer and socialist who established cooperative communities in Britain and the United States. New Harmony, in Indiana, failed after repeated disagreements among its members.

order. The social division lags behind and insists on forcing itself on the productive forces, which causes the latter to be cramped. Then there is revolution and a new class.

Cole would have to revise his judgment on the middle class. It is not disappearing. He assigns to the technical middle class a leading role and says the technical middle class is ready for a long social journey. I think they are not ready for social journeys. The middle class is more capitalistic than socialistic. They would rather protect what they have than to take a chance on a new order.

Cole is trying to salvage as much as he can from Marx. He is modernizing Marx. Cole's book is not a very good book. He is an able man. He writes a lot. Cole is highly reputed, but he is not a clear thinker nor a satisfactory thinker.

I think the most effective program of the New Deal is in giving serenity to the middle class and keeping them from jumping over the traces.

DISCUSSION 5
Social Change
Criticism of the Blueprint Method
The Direction of the Future
How Facism Is Recognized
Differing Theories of Imperialism

I distrust the blueprint method of effecting social change due to (1) the inability of blueprints to get people to follow them. Blueprint people fail to take into account the prejudices of people; they assume the average man is ready to gamble everything he has on a blueprint. From a study of history one finds that the average man wants to be offered an amelioration in adjustment to a life already made. The blueprint approach which appeals to the intellectual has a frightening effect on the average worker. He is asked to put everything on one card—he is afraid—he will not take the risk. This distrust is taken advantage of by vested interests, and they heap up prejudices upon the proponents of blueprints. That is one reason why I do not view the blueprint idea with much hope. Also (2) the blueprint overlooks an important factor in the case. Blueprinters usually seize on one thing and leave out other things that are important. In ninety-nine cases out of a hundred when a blueprint is tried out what you get is something entirely unforeseen. Something of great importance is always overlooked.

Direction. I believe the direction in which we are moving is already decided. The only question is the holiness of it. There are two poles—individualism or collectivism. Social society is based upon the individual pole or the collective society's opposite pole. What decides where a particular society is at a particular period—where the point is between poles—is the state of economic opportunities.

The cartel is a capitalistic guild. When a capitalistic society shows symptoms of oversupply you find capitalist businessmen reverting to group control. The first symptom was the cartel, but then the government came in. Then there were compulsory cartels, and the government enforced economic regimentation. That was the trend of things in the last twenty or thirty years. The free trade of the nineteenth century came to an end; there was a return to government control of foreign trade and internal trade. It was the consequence of the economic contraction of opportunity. Instability in the capitalistic system itself was one factor. Also nationalism and democracy (the endowing of the economic lower classes with political power) was another factor. In the nineteenth century when the capitalistic system got out of gear, who suffered the most? The farmers, small businessmen, and labor.

In our own day, as a result of the organization of masses of people, it became possible for them to refuse to bear the burden of progress and readjustment, and it meant that the businessman's point of view ceased to be the dominant one. The point of view of protecting the trade union, et cetera, came to occupy a high place in determining the policy of the nation. A chronic state of affairs existed, and the expansion of the optimistic did not prevail any more. *Laissez faire* is over—individualism is over—because the lower class refuses to bear the burden as it did in the nineteenth century, and big business runs to the government as to a mother.

The direction in which we are going is no longer an issue. We are going in the direction of an *integrated economy*. The government is in the picture and sees to it that the legitimate expectations of the people are given. The question remains, Who is going to put it through? The fascists or the New Deal organization? Who will occupy the driver's seat?

I prefer a push from behind rather than an alleged pull from the blueprint. The push is not just an economic one, but also an ethical civilization push from behind. It is human rights and so on. The push from behind is not only an economic necessity but also an urge for freedom and heritage. We may lose it all if the fascist gets the seat of power. If we are mindful of danger we are in a better position to deal with danger by dealing with real things instead of theories.

How are we to recognize fascism when we see it? A dead-sure symptom that gives it away is the destruction of the freedom of association and as a consequence the extinction of the freedom for groups to choose their own leaders.

Under fascism there is only one governing hierarchy, which is the party. If in society there is a rival power organization, that is a symptom of non-fascism.

Lewis is the leader of the United Mine Workers, but there are other powers. The employers fight him. The existence of other power organizations act as a check. John L. Lewis does not permit the coal miners to freely exercise the franchise in the offices of the United Mine Workers, but he knows he must give wages, and so on. He is a political tyrant, but he knows the members submit because economic necessity is their potent interest.

Two symptoms of non-fascism: (1) the existence of free associations, and (2) the pluralism of social power.

Is the United States immune to the monopolism of social power which is fascism? The instrumentalities—you have to dispose of government, have a centralized government to dispose and control. The instrumentality of a unified physical force (army, police) does not exist in the United States. (In Germany there is a structurally centralized police operation.) Short of a disastrous war—I am rather at ease about the whole thing.

The average American does not have much faith in the government as a savior. In America there is local vigilance. If an economic collapse—or local disregard of law and order—there will be local vigilance. There was a self-righteous protest in the interests of the farmer eight years ago. It is hard to think of the local forces fused into the nationwide. We are not accustomed to act as a nationwide movement. We resort to local action.

I am banking on the Irish population of the United States. It would be a tough job for the Fascists to coerce them.

After the war we are going to be, apparently, leaderless. I see no one on the horizon to step into Roosevelt's shoes.

Imperialism: Kautzky's theory of imperialism—a program to avoid war and revolution. How to avoid war? Integrated imperialism—under which ruling classes of countries agree to divide and not go to war. (International capitalism—international order.) Kautzky—capitalism has been preparing the framework of international order, which makes war unnecessary. In each country the proletariat through political means will have democratized government and have international democratic order—capitalistic.

This upset Lenin, because the capitalistic system in all countries was not uniform. International order was impossible because the capitalistic countries could not agree due to the varying tempo of development. According to Lenin an international capitalistic order could not come to be because it was fraught with war. He also brought out that Kautzky made a definition of imperialism. He turned the whole thing on the political. He made it turn on the political or the governmental aspect rather than an economic interpretation. Lenin accused Kautzky of having deviated from the Marxist approach. Lenin felt moral indignation and deliberate betrayal.

When you talk of imperialism, would you say it is Lenin's interpretation of imperialism—that imperialism and war stem from rival capitalistic interests? Does that satisfy you? For our own day?

My term is plebeian imperialism. I used it in lectures last year. The Nazis today are the master race. It is not just success but the real thing they are after.

The question today is, Is imperialism finance capital imperialism or can it be political imperialism?

The Leninist-Marxist concept is that imperialism comes from finance capital. (Writers point to fascism as capitalism and thus black the eye of capitalism. But it has turned out that more people like the capitalists than we think; thus it did not black the eye of fascism.)

We have a tendency to think of imperialism as finance capitalism and of German imperialism as such, and to believe that in time there will be a revolt in Germany because the people will not fight. Thus we are lulled by our intolerant idea of imperialism. The German regime is strong imperialism. It is an imperialism that stems from political imperialism—the German idea of a master race.

DISCUSSION NOTE: Assigned reading was H. B. Parkes, *Marxism: An Autopsy.*

DISCUSSION 6
*A Résumé of Paul Crosser,
"Ideologies and American Labor"
Perlman Evaluates Cole and His
Program for Effecting Socialism*

We have seen that from Crosser's three ideologies[1]—(a) harmony in the estate, (b) balances in the market, and (c) class struggles—he discovers three kinds of unionism: paternalistic, business (bargaining), and class struggle (revolutionary). He identifies these in the American labor picture. He does not view the problem from the standpoint of a labor leader—the movement aspect is ignored. He looks at it as a detached observer. It is theoretical. His attitude is that struggle is determined by the circumstances, and it is simply a matter of who wins the struggle. If capitalism in the Marxist sense is accepted there is no way of escaping except by crises and struggle. The book has a Marxist cast: a historical approach using class theory.

Cole is a practical socialist. He was an advisor to the Labour Party in contrast with Crosser, who is ideology conscious. What is Cole's program for bringing socialism in?

Labor is moving up into the middle class—there is a new middle class of technicians and specialists (salaried). (The old middle class consisted of landowners and entrepreneurs.) The middle class has a preferred place in the social structure. It is not likely to get together with the proletariat because this would endanger the preferred position. Fascism is also a possibility, then uniting with the grand bourgeoisie.

1. The discussion had begun with a student résumé of Paul K. Crosser's *Ideologies and American Labor* (New York: Oxford University Press, 1941).

Cole does not think that by means of the ballot socialism can maintain its position. It should get into office constitutionally. Then go to the limit of the socialist program. For if it keeps to democratic processes, the mistakes of the laborers would be capitalized on by the opposition, and the laborers would be turned out.

Cole objected to the gradualness of the labor program. He thought that by announcing a strong program and by government they could wear away many members of the new middle class. The promise of strong action would be the seducer.

American labor has taken over the railroads, which are not run in the interest of owners, but in the interest of shippers and labor.

Cole wanted labor and the new middle class to get together and speedily abolish the capitalist system.

Technicians resent the ascendancy of trade union leaders, who come from unskilled labor. They have a middle-class bias against power in the hands of "lower class" members.

What would be the political result of labor demands in technocracy? Engineers are efficiency minded. Under capitalism the need for efficiency makes engineers impatient with trade unionism, which is by necessity inefficient.

Cole overlooks the essential role played by politicians in any society as a buffer between classes and groups. They are mediators between interests and factions. This conceives of politicians as neutral. Is this the case? Or at least, what happens when you have a leader with political talents and a positive program?

A promise of drastic institutional changes would alienate many votes, labor as well as the middle class. The New Deal method is the best system. This requires skillful politicians. I assume that there are classes and that they have interests which only politicians can reconcile. We are going to get institutional changes by being pushed from behind; by solving problems.

DISCUSSION 7
*A Résumé of Franz Oppenheimer,
"The State"*

In his book, *The State,* Oppenheimer discusses theories of the state.[1] He says that state organization is political cohesion and everyone in history was or is in a state of classes. In emphasizing the importance of land he points out that the class state arises only where all fertile acreage is occupied completely and

1. Franz Oppenheimer, *The State, Its History and Development Viewed Sociologically*, trans. by John M. Gitterman (Indianapolis: Bobbs-Merrill Co., 1914).

says that at present all land is occupied economically, meaning it is preempted politically. Land is preempted by the ruling class against the subject class.

Oppenheimer's discussion of the genesis of the state stresses that there are two means by which man gets what he wants, and that is by work and robbery. He calls one's own labor and exchange of one's own labor for labor of others the "economic means," unrequited appropriation of labor of others the "political means." History, he says, is a contest between economic means and political means, and it can present only this until there is free citizenship.

He believes the state will cease to be political means and will become a freeman's citizenship. When the content of the state changes there is the disappearance of economic exploitation of one class by another. The state of the future is a society guided by self-government of no class or class interests. The state is political means and society is economic means. In a freeman's citizenship there is no state but society.

The development of the state is a battle between political and economic means. Economic means win in the end. There will be well-being but no wealth.

He thinks the future program of nations will be in the direction pointed out by liberal socialism. He contends that we can and probably will establish a society free from all monopolistic tendencies by unfettering competition, which today is far from free. He says competition in our present society is a powerful class monopoly not created through economic differentiation, as up to this time students have believed, but through political power. This class monopoly stands between man and land, and so a laboring class was established which may be influenced by the upper classes because it is not in control of the means of production necessary for carrying on its work in its own interest.

His theory is that there are two ways of acquiring the world's goods—by economic means and political means—and hitherto most people preferred the latter method of becoming rich. The instrument of accomplishing this was the state, and it did so by enabling the stronger to appropriate to themselves other people's labor, principally through the institution of private ownership of land. Every state is founded on the subjugation of some peaceable community without politics by some warlike neighbor. Conquerors become the ruling class and continue to amass wealth by politics while the subject tribe toils and gives to the rulers. Some states start in a different manner, such as the United States, but here, too, there are subject and ruling classes. All states are class states. There is progress in the direction of the substitution of economic for political action until the latter has disappeared and with it the state.

The ultimate goal, according to Oppenheimer, is the abolition of the state and the substitution of a freeman's citizenship. Here people will act according to economic methods and every kind of compulsion, such as we associate with the state, will have disappeared.

Oppenheimer has the robber-baron idea. An unanswered question is, How will the method of economic means overcome political means? Oppenheimer does not stress method as Marx does.

DISCUSSION 8
A Discussion of H. B. Parkes,
"Marxism: An Autopsy"

Having read Parkes' book *Marxism: An Autopsy*[1] and his proposal, I think
Parkes is a left-wing Catholic. I have this idea because he is distrustful of the
state. He is antistate. He says create economic organizations functioning on
their own to counteract the tyranny of government. The left-wing Catholic
ideal relationship of labor and capital is a cooperative workshop. Parkes would
make the worker's job his property. The Catholic idea of reunion of ownership
and labor is to go back to the Middle Ages. Individualistic isolation of the labor
problem. The progressive Catholics in recent years have advocated distribution
of profit sharing. Give labor proprietary interest. Parkes' idea recognizes the
new type of property—property of the job—and that gives the worker a proprietary interest, brings it into a cooperative relationship. It is a partnership
idea (do away with the proletariat). The Catholics say do away with the proletariat because it has no property. Why are they for property? Because it has
a stabilizing effect on humans.

Unionism comes to mean that the ownership of the job is taken away from
the employer and goes to the individual and the union.

Where does Parkes diverge from the union idea? He is close to the union
idea by the idea of the job as property. He departs from the union idea of the
standard wage. His idea is that wages are flexible. The union has the idea of a
standard rate and defends it—the strike, and so on. The unions are willing to
take unemployment in order to maintain the wage rate. Unions do not want
a flexible rate. For a time they viewed favorably the idea of the "sliding scale."
It ties the price of the wage to the price of the product. In 1865 there was a
sliding scale agreement of iron masters and puddlers—the wage went up and
down with the price of iron. Unionism gave it up. Another concept of theirs
is the "standard of living." There was another attempt at a sliding scale after
the First World War. The wage was tied to the cost of living (it was used in
Canada the most); it was tried in the printing trades, but it broke down. They
want to maintain their rate; the idea is that that rate adds to the workingman's
"face." Attachment to rate is a union precept and they fight for it on the
ground that it is difficult to raise the rate—once you have it, hang on to it.

1. Henry Banford Parkes, *Marxism: An Autopsy* (Boston: Houghton Mifflin Co.,
1939).

I reviewed the book for the *American Economic Review*. The book is a throwback to the sixties and seventies in the labor movement, a throwback to the Greenback scheme to do away with the wage system and let the producers have cheap credit, and to do away with private capitalism.[2]

Conclusion: Parkes' idea was not influential because he was Roman Catholic and because of his remarks about Mexico. He probably used Jefferson and Jeffersonianism. He did cite Jefferson.

Critical part of Parkes' book: The first part of Parkes' volume is a closed view of Marxism, an autopsy of Marx. He makes a distinction between social determinism or social conditioning and economic determinism or economic conditioning; that is, social conditioning is accepted but economic is just one theory—economic conditioning—economic one of many factors.

DISCUSSION NOTE: Assigned reading was A. M. Bingham, *Insurgent America*; S. Perlman, *A Theory of the Labor Movement*; and Donald Nelson's statement in the *New York Times* of March 25, 1942, on the Smith-Vinson bill to repeal the forty-hour week. In referring to the latter, Professor Perlman observed that the wartime bonus—overtime—was a wise thing and better than a high hourly wage which would hold over after the war.

DISCUSSION 9
A Discussion of A. M. Bingham, *"Insurgent America"*

A. M. Bingham's real purpose in *Insurgent America*[1] is to figure out a program for the future—how to sell socialism to America, an economic system based on production for use and not for profit.

2. Professor Perlman in his views of Parkes' book states, ". . . a throwback to the 'greenbackism' of the sixties of the past century with its ideal of the escape from the wage system in 'self-employment' *via* the cooperative workshop buttressed up by an access to 'free capital.' The author does not explain how he would solve the management problem in these cooperatives." "Reviews and New Books," *American Economic Review* (March 1940), pp. 130-31.

1. *Insurgent America: Revolt of the Middle Classes* (New York and London: Harper & Brothers, 1935).

Bingham accepts the trade unionism theory of labor—conservative. According to Bingham, labor is out of it. From labor he goes to the middle class—this is a middle-class country. A member of the middle class is anyone who thinks of himself as in the middle class. Bingham thinks the middle class is a psychological category. (Source of income is not decisive as to whether middle class or proletariat.) Neither source of income nor the size or level of income is decisive. Bingham tries to give a psychological characterization of the middle class. He brings out that America is a middle-class country. Attributes of *American middle-class spychology*: property, morality, security, stability, belief in progress—life is getting better and fuller all the time, the national horizon is bounded only by itself.

Bingham describes the middle class as being optimistic and then gives himself a large order—to convert the middle class to a socialistic order of things. To take up from the old landmarks and go to socialism. He invites the American middle class on a long social journey. Does that jibe with his idea concerning security which he applies to the middle class?

The New Deal policy is quite different from Bingham's. Bingham—a Utopian or fanatic when he puts his program before the middle class to follow on a long journey.

I am doubtful if Bingham's program, production for use, will work.

DISCUSSION 10
Some Comments on James Burnham, "The Managerial Revolution," and Perlman's "Theory of the Labor Movement"

After the war Dr. Witte[1] and I think the hatred of the American will turn toward Washington and centralization.

Burnham, in his *Managerial Revolution,*[2] shoves aside the corporation politician and says there will be replacement by the bureaucrat, the government official, and the technician. He misapprehends where power really comes to rest. It does not rest with technicians. I think power is the politician or dictator

1. Edwin E. Witte (1887-1960), Professor of Economics, University of Wisconsin, Madison.
2. James Burnham, *The Managerial Revolution* (New York: John Day Co., Inc., 1941).

type (who also is a politician). The politician understands human nature. I am using the word politician in the European sense. In England politicians are not despised. The politician is a person who knows how to frame policy aiming at a concrete objective and human reaction. A politician is a practical psychologist—in dictatorship, a politician dictator. That is where power gravitates—it is leadership. John L. Lewis is in the doghouse now, but he has leadership. He is an industrial politician. He is a leader of man and not a technician. A technician is not fitted to lead men. He knows too much. His plans and policies are mechanical. I do not think much of the book *The Managerial Revolution.*

In public life it is the politician rather than the public administrator who is important. You have to have the politician. It is my idea that in our society the normal power of formation is held by the politician. As Al Smith did as a politician—he had intellectuals, used their ideas, but filtered them through his mind and then presented them.

People say a business executive but really mean a politician. It is the industrial politician or businessman who decides if the technician's plan is too perfect, and so on. Power gravitates or is wielded by the politician type who understands human beings. Decision is his; whether to follow the technician's plans or not. The industrial politician is a fair-haired boy and he can make mistakes and people will forget.

The American tradition is anti-bureaucratic and anti-technician. People resent lawyers and doctors, and so on—they do not want to give them power. Businessmen's control is not resented. If businessmen do overstep there is resentment but it is soon forgotten. They can readily get back into American public favor.

Technicians do not rule in Russia. Stalin played to the technicians but did so to wipe out his rivals. *Story.* Prior to 1934, when purges in the party began, the engineer packed his suitcase and was ready if arrested at night. After 1934 he quit packing his suitcase—but the politicians packed. Stalin is a politician.

As I understand the process of power formation it concerns the politician rather than the technician. An example is Goering, who is a politician.

I do not think you can train for leadership—people have it or they do not have it. You cannot train for leadership. Schools can merely add to natural abilities.

You can train for public life, for technical jobs, but not for leadership. My book, *A Theory of the Labor Movement*, was written in 1925 and 1926 and published in 1928. At that time there was great talk of banker control. The question is within the capitalistic group itself. I will read from my book.

> The opportunity for unionism to produce a change of attitude
> among the employing group is vitally affected by the shifting of
> power within that group itself. Ownership and management are
> becoming more and more divorced. The wide distribution of the

stock of the giant corporations of today has created what has been aptly termed a "stock holding proletariat." When such a corporation is first formed, usually by purchase of several going business units and a consolidation of their plants and organizations, involving enormous original flotations of securities, control gets lodged in the hands of investment-bankers, who appoint the board of directors and determine the election of the head managers. This is "banker control" of industry, which, in labor and radical circles, is held to be highly detrimental to the cause of unionism, although it is questionable whether bankers as bankers have a stronger prejudice against unionism than have other big businessmen, or whether they will act upon that prejudice more consistently.

But the evil of banker control as absentee control by the financier, himself divorced from actual management but dictating absolutely to management on the ground, has been greatly exaggerated. When the new corporation has proved a success, especially when it has been able to provide the capital necessary for expansion out of its earnings, or where its credit rating is so exceptional that it can sell stock directly to the public, or "over the counter," as it were, banker control is naturally at an end. Power then solidifies in the hands of professional managers, themselves with little or no stake in the business as investors, but with a momentous stake of a different order—the stake of their reputations as successful business managers. These professional managers, so long as the stockholders receive their dividends, usually enjoy an unhampered discretion in arriving at decisions, together with an assured tenure of office. They form, in other words, a business aristocracy not unlike the feudal aristocracy of old. It is very questionable where this aristocracy of managerial executives is by nature any less intolerant of the unionist *demos*, with its "common rules" and restrictions, than is an aristocracy of absentee bankers. On the contrary, the immediacy of its contact with unionism, compared with the remoteness of the bankers, would appear to make it even more impatient with union restraints upon the employer's freedom. Yet such has been the course of American business that it is to the satisfaction of this managerial aristocracy that unionism must demonstrate its capacity to transform methods developed in a prolonged struggle to wrest job control from a greedy and exploitative capitalism, into an efficiency technique of union-management cooperation, superior even to that of the "company union." And, to add to its difficulties, unionism must perform this *volte-face* in the matter of efficiency while safeguarding the workers' ability to wage a fight against the employers if driven to it. The "new wage policy," solemnly adopted at the convention of the American Federation of Labor in 1925, promised exactly this *volte-face*. While enlarging labor's claim upon industry from a "fair" wage to a share in the proceeds of its progressive efficiency, labor pledged itself, by implication, to an unstinted cooperation towards bringing that efficiency about. In making this pledge, the Federation did no more than approve for general adoption the justly famous Baltimore and Ohio plan of union-management cooperation which, in the four years of its operation, and applying to the shop crafts on that railroad— permitted to continue as integral parts of their respective national unions, acting through their national officers—has proved to work far better than a company union plan. The same anxiety to pass muster before the managerial group is shown, lastly, in the renewed efforts to settle old and troublesome jurisdictional disputes in the building indus- try, and in the readiness displayed by several unions in that industry to join the organized employers in a constructive disposal of the appren- ticeship question.

Finally, whether or not unionism will eventually, by modifying its own methods, succeed in outflanking the new strategy of capitalism, there can be no doubt as to the seriousness, for its future, of the recent metamorphosis of the "supply and demand" species into "welfare capi- talism."[3]

For unionism to survive in the twenties, the big corporations do not need to go to Wall Street; they could raise their own capital out of profits. Wall Street lost its controlling influence—not banker control, but management control. But management control is not pro union—the manager is scrappy. Tom Greider fought the union.

I will read what Stolberg said in 1929 since he came to my view of labor.

Professor Perlman starts by probing into the very beginnings of his own mind in the theory of labor—with a confession. ...

Professor Perlman's theory itself is very simple. If he himself were simple, it would be almost simple-minded. There are, to him, two irreconcilable views in modern labor. There is the false, impractical, "intellectual," and bad Hegelian obsession that labor intrinsically wants a new society. Then there is the sensible, sound, and good view of labor as a business method in collective bargaining. This theory Dr. Perlman applies to the Russian and German revolutions, to the British labor movement, and to American trade unionism. Under his expert guidance the theory proves that industrial liberty is commensurate with plain trade unionism, whose strength is in inverse ratio to social-democratic doctrine. This makes the unadulterated and anti-intellectual business unionism of the American Federation of Labor the finest expression of labor freedom. Professor Perlman traces and defends this point of view with much astute and skilful learning

3. Selig Perlman, *A Theory of the Labor Movement* (New York: Macmillan Co., 1928), pp. 216-18.

and with an amazing sensitiveness to all the winds of doctrine. The sidelights he throws on the development of modern labor are often brilliantly provocative. The only thing that's wrong with the theory is the point of view itself. It is historically false, psychologically untrue, economically wrong, and contemporarily not so. A labor movement is alive to the degree to which it is impregnated with a social-democratic drive. And the American Federation of Labor is petty, impotent, ignorant, and frequently corrupt, because its philosophy is to be a job trust.

Then why does a man of Professor Perlman's singular intelligence develop and defend such a "theory"? The answer is that this book is really, as its first sentence pinpoints, an "apologia pro vita mea" rather than a study in "social economy. ... For if you know enough of labor to discard his theory of it, you will appreciate that for all his fears he has written one of the best books on it since Hoxie's study of trade unionism."[4]

Harold Laski's review of my *Theory of the Labor Movement* appeared in 1929.[5]

There is the nucleus of job interest and the exploitation of organizations in order to protect job interests. They (labor) will experiment with legislation and such. This did not lead to a labor party because they can effect more by political pressure.

The book emphasis. Intellectuals think in abstract terms, blueprintish, and give labor all kinds of proposals which expose job interest to hazards, risks, and so on; but labor will not listen to them because the job is her child. British labor since 1928—the radicalism from Cripps, who wanted labor to chase out Chamberlain and unite with the communists, and adopt a stand against Hitler. Cripps was expelled from the Labour Party. Labor did not want to assume office—they knew they could not swing it. For labor to assume office (this was around 1938)—Cripps urged labor to assume national leadership in a strong foreign policy—they criticized Chamberlain but did not want his office because they felt they could not swing it. So they looked to Cripps as an affliction because he exposed them. The British labor movement did not depart from the experimental approach and rush into radical things.

DISCUSSION NOTE: Assigned reading was Selig Perlman, *A History of Trade Unionism in the United States.*

4. Benjamin Stolberg's review, "An Intellectual Afraid," of Selig Perlman's *A Theory of the Labor Movement* appears in *The Nation* (June 26, 1929), pp. 769-70.

5. Harold Laski's review of *A Theory of the Labor Movement, Weltwirtschaftliches Archiv*, Zeitschrift des Instituts für Weltwirtschaft und Seeverkehr an de Universität Kiel, Herausgegeben von Bernhard Harmes, 29 (1929), 220-22.

DISCUSSION 11
Contemporary Observations of
Production and Labor

In his book *The Unfinished Task,* Lewis Corey[1] wants to take private monopolies and reorganize them as public corporations with freedom of action, and management is to play a leading role. He does not say how management is to be implemented. Labor is represented on boards but it is only a minority. Management is to go into the open market—free market connections.

It is a clever book and good in elucidating the process of power formation, but his own positive program, his public corporation is not so clear.

I have a letter from my assistant, who is in Washington on the War Production Board, that I will read to you. Evidence shows that bitterness is growing against labor in the United States. In the classroom we assume a natural transmission from the trade agreement to the cooperative phase—union and management cooperation. This is being kind. We generalize about this for industry.

We have forced a growth in a few years which had taken England thirty years or forty years to do. That means a soreness. Now there is production drive, and we confine ourselves to slogans and the like. Unions think along national lines. Management today is afraid of encroachment by the unions.

The problem now is production, and employers are hindering it by their fear of the sovietism of industry. There is agitation, hatred of Roosevelt, and so on. It is important to be productive. Speeches are made about it.

The Reuther plan was introduced as a criticism of existing companies. The plan was to nationalize the execution of production, and labor was to sit in on it. This was criticized as labor trying to crash management.

DISCUSSION 12
An Elaboration by Perlman of the
Emphasis in His Book "Theory of the
Labor Movement" and an Analysis
of Stalin's Leadership

Labor adjusts itself to the environment and tries to change the environment. The basic idea of my book *A Theory of the Labor Movement* was that the Russian Revolution was a unique phenomenon not to be reproduced in West-

1. Lewis Corey, *The Unfinished Task: Economic Reconstruction for Democracy* (New York: Viking Press, 1942).

ern countries. The Russian Revolution was put through by a relatively limited group of revolutionary intellectuals inspired by Marx and Lenin, and they were able to do so because of the lack of resistance of bodies of society. The theme of the book is the impossibility of communism in the Western countries because the Russian structure is different from the Western countries.

Under certain conditions in certain countries, where organic groups are not strongly developed, the seizure of power of a small group can work. I was in Italy in 1906–7. It was a liberal country—a good place to live—no strong hand anywhere. An "amorphous" country. Of millions only forty or fifty thousand were interested in politics—really citizens. Mussolini could succeed. In Russia there was a lack of political consciousness, and the Lenin group succeeded. Factory workers are the tailor-made proletariat.

The keynote of the book Russia on one hand and West Europe and the United States on the other are two divergent social structures. One is amorphous and a small group of revolutionaries, and they shape the country. In other countries it could not be done. When you applied "Russia" to other countries it failed. In the United States there was no chance for revolution in 1933.

The emphasis in the book is upon the organic groups in our society that weighed themselves against each other in the social scale. Subject to the outcome of war is the tendency of groups to find their own place. In Western society the middle classes are important. When the conservatism of labor gets going it is impossible to have a communistic revolution.

This was true before Hitler got going. To what extent has it been modified?

The emphasis of the book is that the forces of conservatism are stronger than radicalism. The conservative weight is wielded by traditional conservatism, such as the view which the countryside takes of the lord, or the tendency of small business to follow big business and for unionism to be relatively conservative. The assumption was that the whole plane of social life has remained more or less as it was in nineteenth-century conservatism—a traditional kind of conservatism as well as leadership—and that precludes a communist revolution.

What happened? I was right in my estimation of radicalism. In Germany the revolutionaries were overthrown. The Communists felt that Nazism would just last overnight. The Communists fought the Social Democrats, the trade unionists. There was no unity in the radical ranks; they yielded without a fight. I was not wrong in giving radicalism the shorter end of the horn.

I had not foreseen a middle-class revolution against civilization. The plane of social process was tilted and old standards went by the board. A new phenomenon appeared—a Nazi system with the old organic groups subjugated and rule in the hands of a military political group. The actual way in which radicalism was defeated, as in a showdown, for example in 1920 and 1923. I thought it was defeated by conservatism, but actually it was defeated by the above new force backed by conservatism.

In the United States. The basic type of unionism stood up. There was a split in the AFL and CIO but the CIO basic unionism was the same—job consciousness. The vision of unionism in the United States has widened. This is true because of the change in the environment. As long as the hinterland of the job is in business then unionism is pure and simple, but since the hinterland has widened and government has entered—the union vision widens to take in the broadened vision.

There is the federal power to regulate labor conditions—it forces employers to bargain—and there is government spending. This appeared in the thirties, and unionism adjusted itself.

The impetus, the change, came from the conditions—changes in the environment. The labor movement was pushed from behind. Labor had new doors of opportunities. The conduct of the labor movement was not expounded by a blueprint but by changes in the environment.

In the indirect method you squeeze out progressivism. Use the direct method and you get it in the neck.

The development of the labor movement since the New Deal bears out the job conscious concept. It is not a static concept but dynamic.

The chief amendment of my theory of the labor movement concerns fascism. I saw the victim, but the executioner was dim. I saw a different executioner. I will not say the executioner was capitalism—that probably would suit my book better; but it is not so—that Nazism is finance capitalism, as Laski says. This theory is better for my book, but I do not think that is so—the idea of capitalism.

The role of the intellectual—I don't think anything that has transpired in the last fifteen years is theirs. They continue to blunder. The intellectuals' approach—dealing with abstractions—is kept up.

In Russia in the last fifteen or twenty years, amorphous—there could be no breakdown because of hunger. The peasants were a dependable meal ticket. In 1930 and 1931 Stalin put through a collective program. In the middle 1920s Trotsky called attention to the village bourgeoisie—the kulaks (fists). The peasant gives grain to others and that makes others work for almost nothing. Trotsky proposed—weaken the kulaks and hasten the industrialization of Russia. He wanted to siphon off the capital of the richer peasants. Trotsky was defeated by Stalin in 1926–27. Stalin then had a five-year plan. When Trotsky said keep an eye on the village and have industrialization, he meant gradually. Stalin did this five and ten times as fast. Stalin put it over, and the people took it. I was astounded that Stalin could do it. It was done, but at a price of a great catastrophe. Stalin was ruthless and a great administrative genius. There were purges during the winter of 1933 and 1934.

The point is that the group that started with Lenin in 1917 and 1918 was later taken over by Stalin. This group of active revolutionaries really created a new Russia. There was an accentuation of Russian nationalism—go back to Russian heroes:

The policy of the Stalin regime fluctuated. Give the peasant more individualism and then take it back again. In 1939 the government cracked down on the peasants again—cracked down on garden acreage, and so on.

From the standpoint of political possibilities what Stalin did is a wonder. The rapid training of the peasant population into an industrial class was astounding. The Russian people are proud of their system and see it as a system with room for talent.

DISCUSSION NOTE: Assigned readings were Selig Perlman and Philip Taft, *Labor Movements* (volume 4 of John R. Commons and others, *History of Labour in the United States*), and Selig Perlman, "U.S.A." (related to the New Deal), in H. A. Marquand, *Organized Labour In Four Continents*.

DISCUSSION 13
A Résumé of Lewis Corey,
"The Unfinished Task"

Let us briefly review the central theme of Lewis Corey's *The Unfinished Task*. It reexamines some old ideals, sucn as individualism is good, government that governs least is good, checks and balances are good.

Corey states that the origin of political democracy is in the class of small proprietors who got independence from property and thus is an effective opposition to the privileged orders. The ideal is to have a separation of economic and political power.

In the first half of the book he discusses the corporate state and discusses fascism and communism and socialism. He then focuses attention on the technocrats and bureaucrats. The observation is made that every emerging setup has a bureau to handle it and that there is a drift toward bureaucracy. The number one fear is a corporate state.

Corey is antimonopolist. The cause of our evils he thinks is monopoly. In the first place, monopolists can dominate domocratic power, and second, they limit production, and third, they cause extremes in business cycles. Corey holds to the theory of unequal deflation. Monopolies reduce employment but protect their profits.

The two parts of the book are about (1) a fear of the corporate state and (2) the dangers of monopoly. Corey says get away from bureaucratic government. The second part presents the idea of trying to instill the idea of democracy into our economy. He recommends that checks and balances be set up in the economic system as in the government. He wishes to set up managed competition.

Corey rejects blueprints and says we should meet day-to-day problems. He says planned economy equals totalitarianism. He thinks complexity—pluralism—is desirable, and expresses a dislike of totalitarian simplicity. He desires to return to the economic morality of the days of *laissez faire*—the dignity of man, that we must have the will to do this.

He believes it is critical to have separation of economic and political power and widespread ownership of property. Corey does not like totalitarian communism. He points out that in prerevolutionary Russia there were forces for fascism and communism—and communism was stronger and thus rose to power. He rejects the state monopoly of all enterprise.

Corey enumerates and discusses the errors of Marx and goes on to discuss what he considers the state's role to be. He enumerates his ideas of some things that are desirable in the social order: (1) we can prevent depressions; (2) we must use an abundance of the technological inventions of the day; (3) it is possible and practical to have more equal distribution of income; (4) it is possible and desirable to decentralize industry; (5) it is desirable to have greater occupational freedom; (6) it is quite possible to give security in jobs, income, and old age, with better medical care and nutrition; (7) we can have much more leisure.

He points out what the forces of industrial democracy are that can end monopoly. He puts great emphasis on cooperatives and labor unions. He also discusses management as a force of industrial democracy.

Corey believes that after the war we are going to have to set up a new industrial order. He proposes an economy he thinks is desirable. The farmer must be independent. He thinks it is possible for the small farmer to compete with large, efficient forces. He is for many little farms. He believes we should democratize democracy. State corporations should take over the huge businesses that cannot operate on a small scale. He cites the TVA as an example of the state corporation, but stresses that it almost runs on its own. Another type of corporation he places hope in is the mutual corporation—credit for small businesses. He places emphasis on cooperatives as playing a function and labor unions as having much to say. Then he presents the idea of an economic court apart from government—all factors involving labor, government, and manufacturing can sue each other if they violate the common law of the economic constitution.

The book is pretty good political science because Corey understands political power formation and has good historic references.

DISCUSSION 14
The Labor Unions' Attitude toward Efficiency

I have received a letter from a friend in Washington. It is about efficiency and causes me to make some observations about efficiency. Management has a spontaneous attitude—management is in charge of efficiency and labor is a good follower. I believe this is the normal attitude of the unions—they are collective bargaining agencies for the purpose of raising standards of employment. The union attitude toward efficiency is not to put it first. First comes the welfare attitude to labor employment; efficiency comes after they are sure standards are not lowered. That is the peacetime attitude. Unions organize for employment standards, and only when they are deeply entrenched do they consider efficiency—thus efficiency is second. Efficiency is not their prime consideration. There is a war on and the government has a drive on to have efficiency. Labor (unions) now says we must be permitted an equal voice with management in solving problems of efficiency and production. Labor does not look at one plant, but takes an industry-wide view. We are for pooling facilities and resources. Unions say we want to be partners with management to get more production. Management is opposed to it—it is afraid of workers' control of industry. The government wants to bring management and unions together in the interest of higher efficiency. The government does not do so directly because management would oppose it, so the government is stimulating company committees. Management is keeping committees as informal as possible and not too many. Unions would like to use the opportunity for coming into management and entrenching themselves in industry in order to take care of the postwar situation. The Bureau is giving international unions information and encourages production time even though it is a plant-by-plant affair—the leader of the Bureau wants unions to throw themselves into it. It has been pointed out this is not the nature of unions—unions use production drives with their own interests as number one and espouse number two. Hence a psychological deadlock in American industry. Each side is afraid. Management is afraid of sovietization and that management will be pushed off the boards entirely. This is not realistic, because labor will not do it. Labor is nervous regarding an antiunion drive after the war like the one in 1921 and 1922. Thus labor wants to use the production drive for entrenching itself in industry more. Each side has fear. The government's first interest is in production.

It is a problem, and it is not a healthful situation. The First World War attitude was better.

Roosevelt is not a good administrator but is splendid in seeing the social and public mind. He is a first-class, well-meaning politician. University people do not realize the need for politicians.

DISCUSSION 15
The Theory of Value and Perlman's
Attitude toward Russia

Coal mining   Value = C + V + S.V.
                                        20 + 70 + 70 = 160

$$\text{Rate of profit} = \frac{70}{90} = 77\%$$

Flour milling   Value = C + V + S.V.
                                        70 + 20 + 20 = 110

$$\text{Rate of profit} = \frac{20}{90} = 23\%$$

$$\text{Rate of S.V.} = \frac{\text{Surplus labor}}{\text{Necessary labor}} = \frac{\text{S.V.}}{V} = 100\%$$

$$\text{Average rate of profit} = \frac{\text{Total S.V.}}{\text{Total C} + V} = \frac{90}{180} = 50\%$$

Production price = (C + V) (1 + rate of profit)
Production price of coal = 90 (1.5) = 135

X = Production price – Value

Coal mining   X = –25

Production price of flour = 90 (1.5) = 135

Flour milling   X = +25

Production price = C + V + S.V. ± X

Coal mining
    Production price = 20 + 70 + 70 – 25 = 135

Dynamics: The falling rate of profits. The individual self-interest of capitalists.
Each capitalist tries to do better than the average.
   The value of a commodity is determined by the time it takes to produce it.
   Value of commodity = three hours of abstract labor time
                        two hours of abstract labor time

Average rate profit 10%. The capitalist wants to do better—reduce hours—
improve machinery.

The dynamics is the individual capitalist competitive spirit.

Keynesian idea—gap in investment—savings.

Marx—attached to metaphysics—a certain essence and entity—a process of
creating labor. He discussed the abstract of labor and the average rate of
profit. It is difficult to establish if Marx was right or wrong.

Hobson is a left-wing economist.

Cole wants to make Marx respectable in economic circles. Cole calls Marx's
theory of value ethical. But Marx is not ethical—his analysis is objective and
subjective.

Marx. Money to him and what it meant is not as it is now. He was a bullionist.
He discussed the intrinsic value of money and the value of bullion. He determined value of bullion by social necessary labor. He was a conservative economist on the money question.

Russian firm currency of 1921–22 was based on gold and foreign exchange.
Russia was one of the first of the countries in monetary distress to rebound
to orthodox economics.

Fascism. The touchstone of Fascism is whether social and economic organizations can elect their own leaders and have free assemblies.

In theory, the Russian system remains true to personality and the ethical
system that Russian socialists in the nineteenth century professed. The Soviet
political framework if permitted to operate gives democratic life.

The Fascist system only degenerated. The Russian did not.

The difference between Russia and Germany is that the Russian growth is
"of something."

Retain an ethical standard and realize hope. In Russia there is an entity, but
at the same time remain critical. Thus be critical and thus a helper of Russia
because if you are not critical people are scared. The more we prove by analysis that the Russian system is different from our own and that we will not
catch it, we head off the fear of the chance to catch it.

My attitude toward Russia. I do not worship Russia but have a realistic
appraisal of the difference between our way of life and theirs and the difference between the Fascist and the Russian. I stress that Russia has a unique
phenomenon—a historical mold. Our government thus can give a freer hand
to help Russia. On the difference between Russia and the United States—let
us be more pro-Russian and understanding than anti-Russian.

EPILOGUE
APPENDICES
BIBLIOGRAPHY
INDEX

Epilogue

A. L. RIESCH OWEN

If, in a chain of knowledge, there is such a thing as a debt to pay or appreciation to be expressed, there may be no better way to fulfill the obligation than by continuing the knowledge, training, and experience gained along the chain. With the publication of this material, I hope that I have helped to perpetuate the "Perlman tradition."

In order to validate a personal evaluation of Professor Selig Perlman and my interpretation of his teaching, it was necessary to learn the opinions of other students of his who are now in academic and public life. Consensus emphasized and re-emphasized the qualities of the man and the value of his courses. Unanimous was the affection, admiration, and characterization of greatness attributed to Perlman; and unanimous was the opinion that course content was rich in factual material, imaginative, challenging, inspirational, and, above all, thought-provoking.

Selig Perlman was a professor of great modesty, generosity, humaneness, and intellectual wealth. He was a great man, scholar, and teacher—one of a caliber too seldom encountered by students. His influence and teaching go far beyond the classroom and intellectual thought into the very character and values of the individual students themselves. Former students testified they were personally and intellectually touched by this man.

The main purpose of this book has been to acquaint students with material, uniquely Selig Perlman's in content and expression, that will both widen and deepen their knowledge of capitalism and socialism. It is also a tribute to a beloved personal friend and teacher.

As colleague and friend, Professor Edwin Witte noted when speaking of Perlman's students, "Almost without exception, they are admirers of Selig Perlman as a man and, generally, ardent supporters of his views." I am one of those students.

161

APPENDIX A

Assignments

PAMPHLETS

Lenin, Vladimir Il'ich. *The State and Revolution.* London: G. Allen Unwin, 1919.

Marx, Karl, and Friedrich Engels. *The Communist Manifesto.* Authorized translation. New York: Labor News Company, 1933, 1939.

BOOKS

Bingham, Alfred Mitchell. *Insurgent America; Revolt of the Middle Classes.* New York: Harper, 1935.

Cole, George Douglas Howard. *What Marx Really Meant.* New York: Alfred A. Knopf, 1934.

Commons, John Rogers, David J. Laposs, Helen L. Sumner, E. B. Mittelman, H. E. Hoaglund, John B. Andrews, and Selig Perlman. *History of Labor in the United States.* 4 volumes. New York: The Macmillan Company, 1918–35.

Lenin, Vladimir Il'ich. *Imperialism; The Highest Stage of Capitalism: A Popular Outline.* New York: International Publishers, 1933, 1937, 1939, 1963.

Marquand, Hilary Adair (ed.). *Organized Labour in Four Continents.* London and New York: Longmans, Green and Co., 1939.

Parkes, Henry Barnford. *Marxism: An Autopsy.* Boston: Houghton Mifflin Co., 1939.

Perlman, Selig. *A History of Trade Unionism in the United States.* New York: The Macmillan Company, 1922.

_____. *A Theory of the Labor Movement.* New York: The Macmillan Company, 1928. Reprints New York: A.M.Kelley, 1949, 1966.

NEWSPAPER

Nelson, Donald. Statement on the Smith-Vinson Bill, *New York Times,* March 25, 1942.

APPENDIX B

Examinations

EXAMINATION FOR FIRST SIX WEEKS

March 18, 1942

For those in odd numbered seats:
   I. Write briefly on the following:
      a. Anarchist view of the state
      b. Utopian and "scientific socialism"
      c. "Foundation" and "superstructure" in the Marxian theory of social institutions
      d. The "Commune of Paris" in Lenin's "State and the Revolution"
   II. In the materialistic conception of history, how do "classes" come to be formed and what determines which shall be the "ruling class" and when?
   III. Does the New Deal conform to Lenin's theory of the state and wherein is the divergence?
   IV. State Lenin's theory of imperialism. Show how the inevitableness of war is a part.

For those in even numbered seats:
   I. Write briefly on the following:
      a. Withering away of the state
      b. Monopoly capitalism and the export of capital
      c. Productive forces and production relations
      d. Ideals and idealists in history making—how each is determined
   II. Give the "life cycle" of a "ruling class" in the materialistic conception of history.
   III. In Lenin's conception, what is the state and why is revolution necessary in the transition from one historical epoch to the next?
   IV. How does the hypothesis of the Nazi imperialism as a "plebeian imperialism" diverge from Lenin's theory of modern imperialism?

164

SECOND EXAMINATION

April 20, 1942

I. Write briefly on the following:
   a. The village commune in Russia
   b. A union of economic power and political power—totalitarian dictator-ship
   c. The Russian factory workers in 1917 a "tailor-made Marxian prole-tariat"
   d. The "job conscious" theory of the labor movement
II. Give Bingham's characterization of the American "middle class" and discuss the feasibility of his plan for enlisting that class on behalf of basic socio-economic reform.
III. a. Why is it important from the standpoint of forming a correct policy towards Russia today to know the true background of the Russian revolution of 1917?
   b. Why were the propertied classes in Russia so weak in the defense of their position?

GRADUATE EXAMINATION IN "CAPITALISM AND SOCIALISM"

May 23, 1942

On the basis of the material handled in this course (lectures, readings, and dis-cussions), formulate a reasoned attitude towards present Soviet Russia of a person whose paramount concern is for the preservation of the way of life in which the system of values revolving around the worth of the individual is per-mitted to strive for effectiveness.

This should include an interpretation of the original Russian revolution, the degree of immunity of the Western countries to a similar upheaval, the evolu-tion of the capitalist social order in the latter countries and the possibility of a *modus vivendi* between the Union of The Soviet Socialist Republic and the non-Soviet world.

APPENDIX C

Bolshevism and Democracy [1]

SELIG PERLMAN, *University of Wisconsin*

...In our own time, when all claims to rule by divine right have at last been relegated to the garret of history, democracy is cherished primarily as a means of effecting peaceful adjustments between opposed groups in society. We look to democracy as our insurance against social upheavals and bloody strife....

...Like any other species it is studied to best advantage in the surroundings of its habitat; so we shall examine Bolshevism in its local and historical setting.

To students of the social sciences it is self-evident that the rule by the proletariat which has now maintained itself in Russia for over two years, in defiance of nearly the whole world, cannot be dismissed as a mere fluke, but must be regarded as a product of Russian life, past and present....

It is an irony of fate that the same revolution which purports to enact into life the Marxian social program should belie the truth of Marx's materialistic interpretation of history and demonstrate that history is shaped by both economic and non-economic forces. Marx, as is well known, taught that history is a struggle between classes, in which the landed aristocracy, the bourgeoisie and the proletariat are raised successively to rulership as, with the progress of society's technical equipment, first one and then another class can operate it with the maximum efficiency. Marx assumed that when the time has arrived for a given economic class to take the helm, that class will be found in full possession of all the psychological attributes of a ruling class, namely, an indomitable will to power, no less than the more vulgar desire for the emoluments that come with power. Apparently Marx took for granted that economic evolution is inevitably accompanied by a corresponding development of an effective will to power in the class destined to rule. Yet whatever may be the case in the countries of the West, in Russia the ruling classes, the gentry and the bourgeoisie, clearly failed in the psychological test at the critical time. This failure is amply attested by the manner in which they submitted practically without a fight after the Bolshevist coup d'état.

1. From *The Problem of Democracy*, Publications of the American Sociological Society, vol. 14 (1920), pp. 216-25.

To get at the secret of this apparent feebleness and want of spunk in Russia's ruling classes one must study a peculiarity of her history, namely the complete dominance of Russia's development by organized government....

Apolitism runs like a red thread through the pages of Russian history....

...But, even after Russian capitalism was thus enabled to stand on its own feet, it did not unlearn the habit of leaning on the government for advancement rather than relying on its own efforts. On its part the autocratic government was loath to let industry alone. The government generously dispensed to the capitalists tariff protection and bounties in the form of profitable orders, but insisted on keeping industry under its thumb.... The bourgeoisie, especially the higher bourgeoisie, could develop only into a class of industrial courtiers. And when at last the autocracy fell, the courtiers were not to be turned overnight into stubborn champions of the rights of their class amid the turmoil of a revolution. To be sure, Russia had entered the capitalistic stage as her Marxians had predicted, but nevertheless her bourgeoisie was found to be lacking the indomitable will to power which makes a ruling class.

The weakness of the bourgeoisie in the fight on behalf of private property may be explained in part by their want of allies in the other classes in the community. The Russian peasant, reared in the atmosphere of communal land ownership, is far from being a fanatical defender of private property....

Just as the bourgeoisie reached the threshold of the revolution psychologically below par, so the wage-earning class in developing the will to rule outran all expectations, and beat the Marxian time-schedule. Among the important contributing factors was the unity of the industrial laboring class, a unity broken by no rifts between highly paid skilled groups and an inferior unskilled class, or between a well-organized labor aristocracy and an unorganized helot class. The economic and social oppression under the old régime had seen to it that no group of laborers should possess a stake in the existing order or desire to separate from the rest. Moreover, for several decades, and especially since the memorable days of the revolution in 1905, the laboring class has been filled by socialistic agitators and propagandists with ideas of the great historical rôle of the proletariat....

...A ruling minority conscious of its perilous situation will inevitably rely on terror to maintain itself in power. Hence there is no occasion for shocked surprise at the bloody methods of the Bolsheviki in 1918. Our assurance that America will be spared Russia's experience ought to spring less from the conviction that Americans would not do what the Russian committee of struggle against the counter revolution has done than from the realization that America is the antipodes of Russia, where the bourgeoisie has no fighting spirit, where the tillers of the soil are half-communistic and willing to forego their natural share in government for a gift of land, and where the industrial proletariat is the only class ready and unafraid to fight. Bolshevism is unthinkable in America, because, even if by some unimaginable accident the government were overthrown and a labor dictatorship declared, it could never "stay put." No one who knows the American business class will even dream that it would under any circumstances surrender to a revolution perpetrated by a minority, or that it would wait for foreign intervention before starting hostilities. A Bolshevist coup d'état in America would mean a civil war to the bitter end, a war in which the numerous class of farmers would join the bourgeoisie in the defense of the institution of private property. But more than that: only a minority in the American wage-earning class is class conscious in the socialist sense of the word.

The typical American trade-unionist is without any ultimate social goal. He is content to endeavor to gain for labor in all industries the same partial control which it already commands in the collective-bargaining industries such as coal mining and building. The social order which the average American workingman considers ideal is one in which organized labor and organized capital possess equal bargaining power....

APPENDIX D

Excerpt from a Letter Written by Professor Perlman

April 19, 1958

To the Conference of Labor Historians
The Tamiment Institute
7 East 15th Street
New York City, New York

Perhaps it would not be improper for me to recall the hesitant advice given me nearly 50 years ago by my illustrious teacher, John R. Commons, when I was fresh from Russia and thought "I knew all the answers" (for had I not pored over Marx, Kautzky and Plekhanov?) that the labor movement of a country was shaped not alone by the factors common to all capitalist countries but to an equal degree by the specific cultural (idealogical) development of its own. Hence we should not expect to emerge with any interpretation of universal validity. He also stressed another point. Keep your interpretation as close to the plane of the empirical events as you can, but never give up searching for the most comprehensive kind of interpretation.

Bibliography

BOOKS AND ARTICLES BY PERLMAN

Perlman, Selig. *A History of Trade Unionism in the United States*. New York: The Macmillan Company, 1922.

——. *A Theory of the Labor Movement*. New York: The Macmillan Company, 1928. Reprints, New York: A. M. Kelley, 1949, 1966. Epilogue for German edition, 1952.

——. John R. Commons, David J. Saposs, Helen L. Sumner, E. B. Mittelman, H. E. Hoagland, John B. Andrews, Selig Perlman. *History of Labor in the United States*. 4 vols. New York: The Macmillan Company, 1918-35. Vol. 2, "Upheaval and Reorganization since 1876," by Selig Perlman; vol. 4, *Labor Movements*, by Selig Perlman and Philip Taft.

——. "The U. S. A." In Hilary Adair Marquand, *Organized Labour In Four Continents*. London and New York: The Macmillan Company, 1939.

—— and William N. Knowles. "American Unionism in the Postwar Period." In T. C. McCormick (ed.), *Problems of the Postwar World*. New York: McGraw-Hill, 1945. Pp. 33-48.

——. "Some Reflections on Russia and the Future of Russian American Relations." Ibid.

——. *Labor in the New Deal Decade*. Three Lectures delivered at I.L.G.W.A. Officers Institute, New York City, 1943-45. New York: Educational Department, International Ladies Garment Workers, 1945.

——. "History of Socialism in Milwaukee, 1893-1910." Thesis submitted for Bachelor of Arts Degree, University of Wisconsin, 1910. 49 Pp.

——. "What Can Americans Do For Russia?" *Wisconsin Alumni Magazine*, 19 (April, 1918), 144.

——. "German Trade Unionism." *American Federationist*, October 1925, pp. 898-903.

——. The following articles in *The Encyclopedia of the Social Sciences* (New York: The Macmillan Company, 1930): "Brisbane, Albert (1809-90)"; "Douai, Adolf (1819-88)"; "Kearney, Denes (1847-1907)"; "Short Hair Movement"; "Sorge, Friederick Adolf (1827-1906)"; "Steward, Ira (1831-83)"; "Swinton, John (1830-1901)"; "Sylvis, William B. (1828-69)"; "Trade Agreements"; "Workers' Education."

——. "The Wisconsin Summer School for Workers in Industry." *American Federationist*, March 1933, pp. 272-78.

——. "Present Day Economic Trends and Their Effect on Jewish Life in
America." *Proceedings of the National Conference of Jewish Social Service*,
May 26-30, 1934, pp. 11-15.
——. "Principle of Collective Bargaining." In *Problems of Organized Labor*,
edited bv Leon C. Marshall. Annals of the American Academy of Political
and Social Science, vol. 184 (1936), pp. 154–60.
——. "Books in the News: Labor." *Saturday Review of Literature*, 17, No. 26
(April 23, 1938), 12-13.
——. "Growing Role of Government as Creator of Jobs, Need for Political
Strength, Dooms 'Pure and Simple.'" *New Leader*, February 28, 1940, p. 5.
——. "Where the News Ends." *New Leader*, August 1, 1942, p. 8.
——. "What's Wrong in American Labor?" *New Leader*, June 5, 1943, p. 5.
——. "Can Labor and the Professors Work Together?" *New Leader*, September 4,
1943, p. 5.
——. "America and Russia After the War." *Wisconsin State Journal,* August 15,
1943.
——. "The New Pan-Slavism." *New Leader*, July 22, 1944, p. 9.
——. "Should the Government Regulate the Trade Unions?" *New Leader*,
September 2, 1944, p. 11.
——. "A Theory of the Labor Movement," February, 1949. 10 typewritten
pages.
——. "What Gompers Bequeathed." *American Teacher*, 34, No. 7 (1950), 8-9.
——, Chairman of Memorial Resolution of the Faculty of the University of
Wisconsin. "On the Death of Ernest E. Schwarztrauber," *Industrial and
Labor Relations Review*, 4 (April 1951), 473-74.
——. "Basic Philosophy of the American Labor Movement." In *Labor in the
American Economy*, edited by Gordon S. Watkins. Annals of the American
Academy of Political and Social Science, vol. 274 (March 1951), pp. 57–63.
——. "L'Istituzionalismo di John R. Commons," *Quaderni di Sociologia*, No. 4
(Turin, Italy, 1952), 191-202.
——. "Jewish-American Unionism, Its Birth Pangs and Contribution to the
General American Labor Movement: America's Social Setting and the Ideo-
logical Evolution of the Labor Movements, General and Jewish." *American
Jewish Historical Society Publications*, 41, No. 4 (June 1952), 297-337.
——. "Jewish Labor, Its Birthpangs and Contributions to American Jewish
Labor Committee." *Outlook*, 1, No. 5 (December 1955).
——. "The Mid-East Crisis and Its Background." Summary of radio talk on
the University of Wisconsin Radio, November 18, 1956, at 1:30 P.M.
——. "A Note on the Political Implications of Proxenia in the Fourth Cen-
tury B.C." *Classical Quarterly,* N.S. 8, Nos. 3–4 (1958), 185–91.

BOOK REVIEWS BY PERLMAN

Cole, G. D. H. *"Short History of the British Working Class Movement*, Vols. I-
III" (1927). *American Economic Review*, 18, No. 2 (June, 1928), 317-19.

Crosser, Paul K. *"Ideologies and American Labor." American Economic Review*, 32, No. 2 (June, 1942), 406-7.

Gilson, May Barnett. *"What's Past is Prologue; Reflections on My Industrial Experience"* (1940). *American Economic Review*, 31, No. 2 (June, 1941), 416-17.

———. *"Report of the Industrial Legislation Commission Union of South Africa"* (1936). *American Economic Review*, 27, No. 3 (September, 1937), 593.

Haider, Carmen. *"Capital and Labor Under Fascism"* (1930). *American Economic Review*, 21, No. 2 (June, 1931), 305.

Hook, Sidney. *"Toward the Understanding of Marx"* (1933). *American Political Science Review*, 27 (August, 1933), 657-58.

Labor articles abstracted. *American Economic Review*, vols. 14, 15, 16, 18, 19, 21, 22, 25, 27 (1924-37).

Palmer, Gladys L. *"Union Tactics and Economic Change: A Case Study of Three Philadelphia Textile Unions"* (1932), *Journal of Political Economy*, 42, No. 6 (December 1934), 849.

Parkes, H. B. *"Marxism:An Autopsy," American Economic Review*, 30, No. 1 (March 1940), 130-31.

Reynolds, Lloyd G., and Charles C. Killingworth. *"Trade Union Publications, The Official Journals, Convention Proceedings and Constitutions, 1850-1941,"*(1944-45), *American Economic Review*, 36, No. 5 (December 1946), 948-49.

Sombart, Werner. *"Der Moderne Kapitalismus"* (1928), *American Economic Review*, 19, No. 1 (March 1929), 78-88.

Ware, Norman J. *"Labor in Modern Industrial Society"* (1935), *American Economic Review*, 25, No. 4 (December 1935), 773-76.

REVIEWS OF PERLMAN BOOKS AND ARTICLES

Bauder, R. "Three Interpretations of the American Trade Union Movement" [Perlman included] . *Journal of Social Forces*, 22 (December, 1943), 215-24.

Calhoun, Arthur W. *"History of Labor in the U.S., 1896-1932," American Sociological Review*, 1, No. 3 (June 1936), pp. 505-6.

Cooper, L. W. *"Theory of the Labor Movement"* (1928), *Quarterly Journal of Economics*, 43 (1928-1929), 164-70.

de Joli, F. P. Geornale. *"Theory of the Labor Movement"* (1928), *Economisti e Rivista d Statistica*, 70 (1930), 8-9.

Douglas, Paul H. *"Theory of the Labor Movement"* (1928), *New Republic*, 60 (August 21, 1929), 23.

———. *"History of Labor—the U. S. 1896-1932, Vol. 4: Labor Movements," American Journal of Sociology*, 44, No. 1 (July 1936), 146-47.

Henry, David. "Comments on Perlman's 'Jewish Unions and Their Influences Upon the American Labor Movement,'" *American Jewish Historical Society*, 41, No. 4.(June 1952), 339-45.

"History of Labor in the United States 1896-1932, IV." *Times Literary Supplement,* January 18, 1936, p. 58.

House, Floyd N. *"Theory of the Labor Movement,"* American Journal of Sociology, 35, No. 1 (July 1929), 137–38.

"Labor Movements," with Philip Taft (1935). *Social Service Review,* 10, No. 2 (June 1936), 382.

Marquand, H. A. *"History of Labor in the United States 1896-1932."* The *Economic Journal,* 46 (1936), 752-63.

Mason, A. W. *"History of Labor in the United States, 1896-1932."* University *of Pennsylvania Law Review,* 85 (June 1937), 863.

Reich, Nathan. "Some Observations on Jewish Unionism; A Comment on Professor Perlman's Paper 'Jewish American Unionism.'" *American Jewish Historical Society,* 41, No. 4 (June 1952), pp. 339–46.

Schneider, Eugene V. *"Theory of the Labor Movement,"* American Journal *of Sociology,* 55, No. 3 (November 1949), 315-16.

Stolberg, B. *"Theory of the Labor Movement"* (1928). *Nation,* 128 (1931), 769-70.

Stolfi, L. *"Theory of the Labor Movement"* (1928). *Bibliofilia facista,* 4, No. 11 (November 1929), 16-17.

"Theory of the Labor Movement" (1928). *Revue Internationale de Travail,* 18 (Geneva, 1931), 327.

"Theory of the Labor Movement" (1928). *Times Literary Supplement,* December 6, 1928, p. 948.

Witte, Edwin H. "Selig Perlman." In "The Theory of the Labor Movement Reconsidered: A Symposium in Honor of Selig Perlman." *Industrial and Labor Relations Review,* 13, No. 3 (April 1950), 335-37.

OTHER MATERIAL CONSULTED

Congressional Record, Senate, August 18, 1959; September 7, 1959.

Ellenbogan, Jack. "Development of Labor Movement Theory," Ph.D. Dissertation, University of Wisconsin, 1954.

Guest Editorial. "The Profile: In His Face, His Books and His Bearing You See It: The World's Trouble is Selig Perlman's Trouble," *Wisconsin State Journal,* August 15, 1943. Portrait included.

Gulick, Charles A., and K. Bers. "Insight and Illusion in Perlman's Theory of the Labor Movement." *Labor Relations Review,* 6, No. 4 (July 1953).

Likshetz, Rabbi Max A. "Dr. Selig Perlman, A Tribute." Beth-Israel Congregation, May 24, 1959. Two typewritten pages.

McGrath, Hazel. "Professor Selig Perlman to End Long, Happy U.W. Career," *Wisconsin State Journal,* May 25, 1959.

———. Feature story from the U.W. News Service, Madison, Wisconsin, released Monday, March 25, 1959.

"Memorial Resolutions of the Faculty of the University of Wisconsin on the Death of Professor Selig Perlman." Document 1401, November 2, 1959.

2 Pp. Signed by Memorial Committee: Walter R. Agard, Elizabeth Brandeis, Harold M. Groves, Mark H. Ingraham, H. Edwin Young.

"Memorial Session to the Late Selig Perlman and Sumner Slichter." *Industrial Relations Research Association Proceedings*, 1959 (Madison, Wisconsin, 1960), 1-19.

"One of U. W.'s Greatest Scholars Prepares for Retirement." *Capital Times* (December 10, 1958).

"Perlman Funeral Eulogy Has Man's Dignity as Theme. Notables at Perlman's Services." *Capital Times*, August 17, 1959.

"Perlman to Take Post at University of Pennsylvania." *Capital Times*, December 6, 1958.

"Perlman Urges Development of Labor. Speaking at Workshop Sponsored by Madison Workers Education Bureau at Labor Temple Saturday." *Wisconsin State Journal*, March 4, 1946.

"A Reappraisal of the Perlman Theory." *Monthly Labor Review*, 72, No. 2 (February 1951), pp. 121-26.

"Selig Perlman Memorial Dinner, University of Wisconsin, November 20, 1959." Cover has excellent portrait and in the background is a portrait of John R. Commons, Ec. Dept. 1904-1936. Introduction, Robert Ozanne, Director, School for Workers; Chairman, H. Edwin Young, Dept. Ec.; Fred Harrington; David J. Saposs, Paper.

Memorial Resolution: Joint Resolution Commending Professor S. Perlman on a Life of Service to Wisconsin, Joint Resolution No. 21A (February 19, 1959), Introduced by Mr. Dueholm.

Stephansky, Ben S. "Selig Perlman on the Role of Labor in a Less Developed Society." *Industrial Relations Research Association Proceedings*, 1959 (Madison, Wisconsin, 1960), 8-14.

Taft, Philip. "Professor Perlman's Ideas and Activities." *Industrial Relations Research Association Proceedings*, 1959 (Madison, Wisconsin, 1960). In all his books and articles, Taft gives a great deal of space to Perlman's work.

Tremblay, Louis-Marie. "La théorie de Selig Perlman: Une étude critique." *Relations Industrielle/Industrial Relations Quarterly Review*, 20 (April 1965), 295-339.

"Tribute to Selig Perlman." From the *Sheboygan Press*, reprinted in *Capital Times*, January 8, 1959.

Index

Agriculture, 75, 78, 106, 108, 109; in early Russia, 65, 69; exports, 76; during the war, 78. *See also* Collectivism; Commune
Alexander II, 68, 74
American Federation of Labor, 153
Anarchists, 77, 90, 91, 92, 95, 98, 99, 101
Artel, 91
Artisans, 79, 80, 81
Austria-Hungary, 24, 45

Bakunin, Michael, 90
Bavaria, 86
Beard, Charles, 128–29
Bebel, August, 49
Bevin, Ernest, 127˜
Bible, 17
Big business, 3, 69, 72, 133
Bingham, A. M.: *Insurgent America,* 145–46
Bismarck, Otto von, 25, 95
Black Sea, 63
Blueprints, 93, 100, 127, 136, 138, 139, 150, 155
Boer War, 45
Bolsheviks, 54, 69, 86, 89, 94, 99, 100, 101, 102, 103, 105, 123, 168
Bolshevism, 165–66
Bourgeois government, 31
Bourgeoisie, 166; the capitalistic class, 10; fitness of, 10; life cycle, 10; morality, 53; revolution, 93, 94–97
Bourgeois revolution, 93, 94, 96–97, 100, 101
Boxer Rebellion, 36
Boyars, 66
Brest-Litovsk, 86, 87, 162
Bull Run, 87
Burnham, James: *The Managerial Revolution,* 134–35, 146
Business, 133; big, 3; Russian, its lack of resistance, 71–72
Byzantine Empire, 14, 64, 67, 132

Canada, 112
Capital: constant and variable, 115
Capitalism: certainties about, upset, 3; British, 4; German, 4; war, 4; Western, 5; support by middle class and trade unions, 5; survival of, 5; structural changes, 35, 61, 119; development of, 37, 39; and Nazism, 43; and fascism, 44; replaced, 56; monopoly, 61, 62; in Russia, 70–71, 101, 102, 106, 166; intellectuals and, 90; and socialism, 90; in cities, 98–99, 105; dynamic theory of, 118–19; changes in, 119; weakened, 120; finance, 141, 153
Capitalist class: beginnings of, 10; replaced feudal nobility, 10; life cycle of a ruling class, 11–12, 14; government. 20–21; fascists, 55; artificial, 73; power of, 131, 133
Capitalistic system, 3, 40
Carnegie, Andrew, 111
Cartel, 138–39
Catherine the Great, 67
Chamberlain, Austen, 109
Chamberlain, Neville, 150
Change: in social system, 3; in Russia, 70–71
Chartist Movement, 28, 131
Chicago, 23
China, 24, 25, 114; Marx-Lenin theory, 31; nationalism, 33–34; Boxer Rebellion, 36, 45
Christians, peasants as, 88
Church, Russian (Greek Orthodox): spiritual life centered in, 65; uprising, 66; split in, 72
Churchill, Winston: leader of England, 6; backed Russia, 6, 111
Civil War, U.S., 110
Classes: ruling and subject, 11; consciousness of, 12; origin of, 15–16; struggle between, 15, 29; identification, 20; economic, 30; leisure, 38
Class struggle, 15, 29, 62

177

DESIGNED BY IRVING PERKINS
COMPOSED BY HORNE ASSOCIATES, INC., HANOVER, NEW HAMPSHIRE
MANUFACTURED BY MALLOY LITHOGRAPHING, INC., ANN ARBOR, MICHIGAN
TEXT IS SET IN PRESS ROMAN, DISPLAY LINES IN GOUDY OLD STYLE

Library of Congress Cataloging in Publication Data
Perlman, Selig, 1888–1959
Selig Perlman's Lectures on capitalism and socialism.
Bibliography: p. 171–175.
Includes index.
1. Communism—Addresses, essays, lectures.
2. Communism—Russia—History—Addresses, essays, lec-
tures. I. Owen, Anna Lou Riesch, 1919–   II. Title.
III. Title: Lectures on capitalism and socialism.
HX56.P38 1976   335.43'0947   74-27312
ISBN 0-299-06780-7